Sigrid Schmidt

Inner harmony through
Bach Flowers

Tried-and-tested remedies to:

- relieve stress at work and in the family

- prevent illness

- promote personal development

TIME-LIFE BOOKS, AMSTERDAM

Contents

Self-treatment with Bach flowers

Important Note

Dr Bach's flower remedies are not a cure-all. On the contrary, critical self-analysis is required before using them in order to find the "right" flower. The Bach flower remedies can act as adjuncts to other therapies in relieving psychological and physical ailments, but the true effect of the flower essences lies in turning negative, burdensome personality traits into positive ones. This book describes the treatment of common ailments with the remedies.

The views expressed by the authors of the HEATLH CARE TODAY series may differ in part from generally recognized orthodox medicine. All readers must decide for themselves whether, and to what extent, they wish to follow any of the advice given in this book on Bach flower essences. Please take careful note of the limits of self-treatment, together with the appropriate remarks on treatment in the text. It is important to stress that seemingly mild ailments may sometimes conceal serious illnesses which must be treated by a qualified medical practitioner. Should you become uncertain regarding the cause and progress of an illness, consult your doctor. Do not take risks – when in doubt, always go to the doctor.

Foreword

This guide is intended to introduce you to Bach flower therapy and I look forward very much to kindling your interest as I explain how to treat yourself with Dr Bach's flower remedies.

Dr Edward Bach developed his therapy more than 60 years ago. Initially, he passed through all the stages customary for a conventional medical training, becoming a Licentiate of the Royal College of Physicians, a Member of the Royal College of Surgeons, a Bachelor of Medicine, a Bachelor of Surgery and a holder of the Diploma of Public Health. However, through his own experience of disease – Dr Bach contracted cancer – his understanding of sickness and health underwent a significant change and he became unable to reconcile his own approach with the methods utilized in conventional medicine. Dr Bach came to recognize that a deep-seated spiritual disharmony, more an unconscious railing at one's own destiny that manifests itself in our everyday conflicts, is the true cause of all illness. In order to treat this spiritual disharmony, and thus be able to prevent illness, he went in search of natural healing substances. Led by deep intuition he found what he was looking for in 37 flowers and in pure spring water. From these, using simple methods, he made his essences.

Dr Bach's flower remedies – the therapy of choice in these hectic modern times fraught with inner and outer pressures – have a harmonizing effect on the spirit. They help us to master the difficult situations we face in our everyday lives, they support us in our ongoing personal development, and they bring us balance when we are ill.

For many years I have treated patients with Bach flower essences and time and time again I have witnessed with joy the astonishing effects they have had. This experience prompted me to write this guide to enable people to treat themselves.

Sigrid Schmidt

About Dr Bach's flower remedies

The wonderful thing about Bach flower remedies is that they afford you self-help support in a simple yet effective way, without requiring a particular talent for or special knowledge of healing. If you can allow yourself to become aware of your feelings and are able to express them in words – for example, whether you are feeling impatient, angry or sad – this is enough to make a beginning with Bach flowers. For every negative state of mind, there is a Bach flower essence that can relieve it.

Before explaining how to analyse your state of mind and find the appropriate flower essence, this guide presents a brief account of how Dr Bach discovered the remedies and the principles upon which he built his flower therapy.

Bach flower therapy

"When I am hungry, I go into the garden and pick an apple; when I am anxious, I take a dose of Mimulus."   Edward Bach

A gentle method

Dr Edward Bach's flower therapy is a natural, gentle method of treatment which enables you to relieve momentary negative feelings and states of mind while advancing your personal development. The therapy will not help you to heal severe emotional imbalances or physical illnesses if these have already caused organic damage, although in such cases Bach flowers could well be effective as support to other methods of treatment.

The following account of Dr Bach's life, his view of people, his perception of the nature of disease and the explanation of how the flower essences were discovered have deliberately been kept as brief as possible and have been greatly simplified. Should you wish to study Dr Bach's thought and the philosophy behind his flower therapy more deeply, you should read his own writings (for additional details see page 100).

Dr Bach's life

Dr Edward Bach was of Welsh extraction and lived from 1880 to 1936. Even during his childhood he displayed great sensitivity and intuition, and his close relation with Nature was remarked upon. As a young man he wandered for hours in the countryside, observing the plants and animals. He was soon able to differentiate between the various species of flowers and grasses even in the earliest stages of their growth.

At the age of 17 Edward Bach began work as an apprentice in his father's brass foundry. Here he was confronted head-on with the hard life of physical labour: because of poor working and living conditions the workers frequently fell ill, and very often they were unable to afford medical treatment. Intuitively, Bach recognized that mental stress was just as much a cause of the workers' illnesses as their physical conditions. He was dismayed by what he saw and felt the need to help in a way that would make medical treatment superfluous, a way that would take effect even before an illness became overt. This early experience may well have laid the foundation stone for Edward Bach's lifelong search for healing substances which would enable people to help themselves.

Mental stress a cause of illness

In 1906 Bach began his medical studies. After qualifying as a doctor, he devoted himself at first to medical research. It was in this period that he discovered a connection between the symptoms of chronic disease and certain strains of bacteria in the human intestine from which he prepared vaccines to cure the diseases; the bowel nosodes.

From 1918 Bach worked at a hospital where homeopathy was accepted and used as a method of treatment. Here he became acquainted with the teachings of Dr Samuel Hahnemann, the founder of classical homeopathy. Encouraged and inspired by Hahnemann's theories, Bach prepared homeopathic medicines from his vaccines, which then no longer needed to be injected but could be taken orally by his patients.

In the course of treating patients with these substances, Dr Bach allowed himself to be led more and more by the patients' moods, their characteristics and states of mind, rather than by their physical symptoms. He went on to attribute particular states of mind to his medicines and used them accordingly. However, he was preoccupied by the fact that the substances he was using derived from bacteria and were not of "pure" natural origin. This provided the impetus to begin his search for plants which would replace the medications he had been using so far.

Discovery of the first flowers

In 1929, on a visit to Wales, Dr Edward Bach found the first three of his flowers and began to treat his patients with them. A year later he gave up his practice in London's renowned Harley Street and went back to Wales to search for more plants. In his search he allowed himself to be guided by his ever-strengthening intuition. Ultimately, he was able to perceive which state of mind could be influenced by a flower just by touching or tasting it.

At the end of his search Dr Bach had discovered 38 essences –
37 flowers plus rock water – which he considered would enable
him to treat all the states of mind he had observed in the course
of his general medical practice.

The foundations of the therapy

Dr Bach's experience led him to turn away from modern medical
science which, in his view, failed to recognize the true nature of
disease. Concentrating as it did on treating the physical symptoms
of disease, he perceived it as treating only the effects and not the
causes of an illness. For Bach the true causes of physical sickness
lay within individuals – in the negative attitudes which people
have towards themselves and towards life, in their character
weaknesses and in their emotional disturbances.

Treatment of causes

Dr Bach's perception of people

Edward Bach's vision of humanity was marked by deeply held
religious beliefs. For him, human beings were creations of God:
perfect, happy, content and healthy. However, through the
circumstances of our lives – experiences in childhood, difficulties
at school and at work, imbalances in relations with others, and so
on – we forget more and more that we are unique beings with no
cause to feel anxious, fearful, desperate or dissatisfied. Likewise, we
forget that within us are innate characteristics which will "direct"
us quite naturally towards the kind of work, profession or lifestyle
to which we are best suited. We forget that we are individuals, each
one of us absolutely unique and comparable with other people
only in the single respect that we are all human beings. However,
in spite of having forgotten all this, we are still human and as such
have not lost our Divine origin, we can simply no longer remember
anything about it.

Coloured by deep religious beliefs

    Forgetfulness on the one hand, and remembrance of our Divine
origin on the other, represented for Edward Bach two diametrically
opposed forces which find expression in the characteristics of each
one of us. For him it was forgetfulness of our ultimate divinity that
gave rise to such characteristics as egoism, dissatisfaction, lack of

courage, susceptibility to outside influences, and sadness. Dr Bach called these characteristics "negative states of mind".
Remembrance, on the other hand, he saw as manifesting itself in courage, understanding, contentment, and love.

The individual's purpose in life

Edward Bach saw the purpose of each individual's life to be the development of characteristics that would enable him or her to be fully and constantly aware of their own individuality. Such self-knowledge and awareness would enable all individuals to set out on the right path in life, to follow it with serenity and determination, and to treat others with understanding while not neglecting their own needs.

The development of positive characteristics

As a rule we are not conscious of our purpose in life. When, at a certain age, we have obtained some experience of ourselves, we can recognize that our emotional life is generally determined by certain recurring circumstances. Thus, according to our personality, we might often feel bad-tempered and anxious, aggressive and dissatisfied, preoccupied and inwardly restless. Dr Bach believed such feelings resulted from a "negative state of mind" and called them "negative emotional symptoms".

None of us should have any difficulty in understanding this connection: we experience situations daily in which we are perfectly aware of a shortage, or even a complete lack, of a particular positive characteristic. How often do we forget our own individuality, or feel inferior to others? How often do we lose sight of our objective, or allow others to talk us into accepting responsibilities which are perhaps beyond our abilities? How often do we lose courage, then become bitter or resentful because our expectations fail to be fulfilled? How often do we insist that we are right, or that something should be done our way, and end up feeling rejected or misunderstood because we should have worked together with others to master a difficult situation?

These "emotional symptoms" show us that something inside us is not as it ought to be. At the same time, they show us the direction in which we should work on ourselves to put things right. Feelings of rejection, of being misunderstood and ignored, are precisely the symptoms connected with self-conceit and

Working on ourselves

egoism. According to Dr Bach, the purpose in life of people who regularly feel these symptoms should be to master their egoism and develop positive characteristics of tolerance and understanding.

Self-discovery   It is often difficult for us, however, to identify precisely feelings like being rejected, misunderstood or ignored: often we are merely aware that we feel vaguely uncomfortable or tense, that we may be reacting in an aggressive way. But even these momentary imprecise feelings can help us on the road to self-discovery if we take notice of them. They can make us stop, take a better look at ourselves and try to see ourselves in the larger framework. In this way we can take up the thread and trace it back, from our momentary feelings, to the inner state of mind from which we often suffer, and finally to the negative characteristic – egoism, hopelessness, lovelessness – which lies at the root of our daily inner conflicts and tensions.

Once we have begun to develop those characteristics that we lack and to overcome our negative ones, we shall find that many everyday moods and feelings will begin to change within us.

Summary

Dr Bach's perception of his fellow humans, which provided the foundation for his flower therapy, may at first sight appear rather intricate and complicated. The following summary might help you to a clearer understanding:

● We are all children of God and share in Divine perfection and harmony.

Negative emotional symptoms   ● Through the circumstances of our lives we develop negative characteristics such as fear, hopelessness and egoism. Dr Bach called these characteristics "negative states of mind".

● Negative states of mind lead to "negative emotional symptoms" such as anxiety, irritability or despair. As a rule, we notice these emotional symptoms over longer periods of time: they are the "emotional atmosphere" which reigns within us.

● These emotional symptoms are expressed in our daily moods and feelings, which are often unclear or blurred, rapidly changing and difficult for us to pin down, such as inner tensions or general feelings of discomfort and disinclination.

This description of the connections between the inner levels of human beings should not to be regarded as a rigid blueprint: the limits between the various areas – the states of mind, their symptoms, and the momentary feelings – are fluid. Thus it can happen that a minor event in the course of a day can suddenly throw your underlying state of mind, for example, egoism, into bold relief. Such a discovery about yourself might come as a shock, but try to remember that it is to your advantage to recognize your inner state of mind: if it is egoism, this could explain any feelings of loneliness which you occasionally feel without knowing why.

Changing moods

Concerning the causes of illness

Dr Bach considered our negative states of mind to be the real causes of any physical diseases which afflict us. Our emotional symptoms, therefore, can serve as signals that a physical sickness is "incubating" within us. For example, constant feelings of anxiety can lead to inner tensions and stresses which disrupt the normal functioning of our organs. In time, such disruption can lead to a stomach ulcer, digestive disturbances or other troubles.

Signals from emotional symptoms

We should not wait until the disease strikes before doing something about it. The actual outbreak of the sickness may lie in the future but the seed has already been sown and will continue to grow so long as we fail to overcome the negative state of mind which feeds it. By working continually on our personal development, therefore, we are at the same time protecting ourselves against physical disease.

If someone is already suffering from an acute or chronic illness, Bach therapy can provide effective support. For when the physical disease is deprived of its "nourishment" – i.e. the person's negative states of mind – it can begin to decrease. Ultimately, with the natural inner healing of the sufferer, the disease could disappear altogether, although such complete recovery would depend on no irreversible damage having already taken place within the body organs or tissues, as is the case, for example, with arthrosis or cirrhosis of the liver.

Support in cases of acute or chronic illness

Relief through flower essences

Healing with natural substances

In accordance with his religious views, Edward Bach was firmly convinced that Nature would have provided a remedy for every ailment known to man, be it physical or emotional. His aim was to find natural substances which would enable everyone to treat their negative states of mind. He developed processes for obtaining essences from the 38 sources he had discovered (see page 15), testing the resulting remedies first on himself and then on other people to confirm their effects.

Taking Bach flower essences can help us to alleviate or even eliminate negative emotional symptoms in many situations, either momentarily or over longer periods of time. If, for example, you are feeling anxious because of an examination you are about to sit, a dose of the appropriate flower essence can relieve this feeling in the short term and make you feel better. Released from your anxiety, you will develop more courage and confidence and probably improve your chance of doing well in the exam. If, however, you realize that you frequently find yourself feeling anxious – be it about a coming examination, an important discussion or interview, a difficult task at work, or a quarrel with your partner – and would like to work on your personal development, regular doses of the appropriate flower essence together with consciously getting to grips with your negative emotion can help you to overcome your anxiety in the long term and even to turn it into courage.

Through taking flower essences in certain situations we can bring about an immediate improvement in our state of mind which will better enable us to cope with the situation. We can also use the flower essences to work on ourselves, to help us develop desirable characteristics which we lack or to temper disruptive ones. Many people who have treated themselves with Bach flower remedies have experienced durable, positive changes in their state of mind.

So far it has not been possible to prove, scientifically or medically, how mental and physical changes are brought about by Bach flower remedies. Even with the help of the most modern technical methods of examination, it has not been possible to trace any active substances in the flower essences. Nor has it been possible to determine any changes in the body's metabolism in a way that can clearly be traced as, for example, after taking an aspirin. We simply do not know, therefore, what actually takes place when Bach flower essences are taken.

How the remedies are made

The manufacture of all flower essences is still done in accordance with the two procedures developed by Dr Bach: the sun method and the boiling method.

How the remedies are made

Sun method

● In the case of the sun method, the flowers are gathered on a cloudless sunny day at the moment of their fullest blossoming and are laid in spring water in a glass bowl. The bowl is left in the full sun for three to four hours, as near as possible to where the flowers were picked. When the blossoms begin to wilt they are carefully lifted out of the water with twigs from the same plant. The remaining liquid is then preserved by the addition of 40 percent vol. alcohol, which is later diluted with spring water to a proportion of 1:20 and stored in "stock" bottles.

Boiling method

● For plants that blossom early in the year, the sun's radiation is not strong enough to capture their essence by application of the sun method. For this reason the boiling method is used. The blossoms, twigs and young leaves of the plant are simmered with spring water in an enamel pan. The process is complete after about 30 minutes, when the flowers have become wilted. The mixture is left to cool and then filtered. It is preserved and diluted in the same way as in the sun method.

Finding the right flower

The "right" flower essence for any situation depends on your individual personality and the particular situation. Both need to be looked at carefully to find the flower or mixture of flowers appropriate for you.

As a general rule, you can discover "your" flower by carefully reading the detailed descriptions of all 38 essences. You will suddenly find – in what could be described as an "Ah-ha!" experience – that you recognize yourself in a description and this identifies the flower to suit you. The following pages offer more detailed guidelines, however, to lead you quickly and surely to the flower that is best suited to you and your situation.

What is your situation? First, take a good look at your situation and decide whether you are experiencing:

- an emergency (see below)
- acute spiritual or emotional stress (see opposite)
- a desire for ongoing personal development (see opposite)
- longstanding emotional or physical disturbance (see page 18)

Now refer to the appropriate section on the following few pages to find the next step. If, for example, you are suffering an emotional crisis as the result of recent separation from a partner, turn to the section entitled "Guidelines for emotional stress" where you will find instructions on the next steps towards finding "your" flower.

Guidelines

For emergency situations

In an emergency situation where immediate help is required in response to a sudden emotional or a physical shock, take the rescue remedy. Everything you need to know concerning the use of this special mixture is in the chapter called "The rescue remedy" beginning on page 98.

For emotional stress

If you have chosen this section, you are doubtless feeling very unwell. In this condition, most people have little difficulty expressing how they feel and so you should find no problems in answering the questions you need to ask yourself in order to select the appropriate flower or flowers.

● Write down on a piece of paper:
   "At present I feel . . ."

then complete the sentence in as many words as you wish to best describe exactly how you are feeling at the moment. If you are using this book and method for the first time the following example may help:

How are you feeling right now?

■ **Example:**
   "At present I feel . . .
   exhausted – sad – despairing – tired – empty – unhappy –
   deserted."

Drawing up a list of symptoms
The list may be bleak, but it reflects the "negative emotional symptoms" you are feeling and as such forms the basis for your choice of flower essences to help you at this moment.

When you have completed your list, turn to the repertory which begins on page 23. Look up the symptoms which currently apply to you and next to them you will find an indication of the flower essences appropriate to that symptom. For more details on how to use the repertory see the section called "The structure of the repertory" beginning on page 19.

For the development of the personality

If you have chosen this section, you are probably among those people who already know themselves pretty well – well enough to recognize your feelings and be able to describe them clearly. In order to further the development of our personalities we must first achieve clarity regarding the main aspects of our natures. Self-questioning can help us to recognize any frequently recurring negative emotional symptoms which could be positively affected by flower essences.

How do you often feel?

● Think about the negative aspects of any moods which you find you are prone to, then write down on a piece of paper:
   "I often feel . . ."

Complete the sentence in as many words as you like to describe the negative aspects of your frequently recurring moods.

■ **Example:**
   "I often feel . . .
   aggressive – impatient – intolerant – unresisting – misunderstood."

Do not be depressed or embarrassed by your list: the characteristics reflect part of your being and will serve as the basis for choosing flower essences to support the development of your personality.
   When you have completed your list, turn to the repertory which begins on page 23 to find the appropriate flower essences. Detailed instructions on using the repertory are in the section called "The structure of the repertory" which begins on page 19.

For longstanding emotional or physical disturbance

If you have chosen this section, you will not have been feeling well, either physically or mentally, for a long time. You will have physical symptoms or emotional problems and are in urgent need of help. To find the right flower remedy for your needs, you must first of all try to determine as clearly as possible which negative emotions or character weaknesses apply to you or cause you difficulty. This is not an easy task; self-questioning will help.

Try to express your feelings in words

● Write down on a sheet of paper:
   At present I feel . . .
   I often feel . . .

Then complete both sentences describing the negative aspects of your state of mind, both at the present moment and in general.

Try to be as honest with yourself as you possibly can – the more precisely you are able to recognize your characteristics and feelings, the better the chosen flower remedies will suit you.

Be as honest as possible

■ **Example:**
"At present I feel . . .
embittered – tired – exhausted."
"I often feel . . .
impatient – embittered – despairing – anxious – envious."

Your lists will describe your current state of mind and also give indications as to your underlying characteristics. Often a feeling will feature in both lists as it describes both your immediate feelings and a regularly occurring mood. When you have finished the lists, turn to the repertory beginning on page 23 to make the choice of flower remedy to help you to feel better. More details on how to use the repertory and given in the section which follows.

Structure of the repertory

The repertory is an alphabetical list of mostly negative "emotional symptoms" and characteristics. It does not claim to be a complete or comprehensive list of all human emotions. The emotional symptoms are in the left-hand column of the repertory and in the right-hand column are the names of one or more flower remedies which are effective against each of the symptoms concerned.

A catalogue of emotional symptoms

The repertory will help you to find suitable flowers more quickly. It makes a pre-selection for you so that you need read only the full description of those flowers you have already identified in the repertory as suitable remedies. Irrespective of this, however, before beginning any therapy it is advisable to read carefully through all the flower descriptions as general background.

How to use the repertory

Before beginning Bach flower therapy you should first read through the repertory thoroughly and get to know it. You will

quickly discover that only one flower remedy is attributed to
certain emotional symptoms, while other symptoms have a choice
of several. This simply means that in some cases only one flower
remedy is suitable to overcome the symptom, while in others
several flowers may be considered.

■ Example:
| Jealousy | Holly |
| Mistrust | Gentian, Holly, Willow |

Some emotional symptoms are sub-divided so that your choice
becomes more precise:

■ Example:
Offended	is easily offended	
	– by lack of gratitude in others	Chicory
	– by a sense of being ignored	Chicory, Willow

If several flowers are suggested, you should read their descriptions
one after the other (see A to Z section beginning on page 39) to
discover which remedy best suits you.

As a general rule, the list resulting from your self-questioning
will contain several negative emotional symptoms and/or
characteristics. Before you start looking them up in the repertory,
check whether there are any words in your list describing your
body or your general appearance.

■ Example:
*"At present I feel . . .
too fat – ugly – plain."*

While such statements are undoubtedly negative, they do not
describe *emotional* symptoms. Rather, they indicate that you are
dissatisfied with yourself. You will not find words such as "too fat",
"ugly" or "plain" in the repertory, but you will find the notion
"dissatisfied" and that is where you should look for the remedy in
this case. Always try to identify the negative emotions
underpinning your list.

Using the list of symptoms

With the aid of the your list of symptoms and the repertory you should now start looking for your flowers. Work through the words on your list, writing beside each one the name of the flowers or flowers you find corresponding to each symptom in the repertory.

Sometimes a word you have used will not appear in the repertory. In this case try to think of other words for the symptom you are describing until you find one which does features in the repertory.

All the flowers that ultimately appear on your list are appropriate to your present needs. Flower remedies that crop up frequently are probably particularly important for you as an individual. But remember that the flowers found through the **Only a pre-** repertory represent a pre-selection and do not necessarily apply in **selection** every case. You should always read the detailed descriptions of the flowers you have identified to discover which of them really suits you best. Try to limit your final choice to six or seven flower remedies; up to twelve is meaningful only the first time you take the remedies (see below).

What to do if something is unclear

It can happen that you find no flower at all that seems suitable, or that you find too many and this makes you unsure of what to choose.

■ **If you do not find a suitable flower**
If you find that none of the 38 remedies responds to your requirements and you feel fit and well, you probably do not need any of the flower remedies at present. However, if you feel unhappy and in need of treatment and still find no flower remedy, your self-diagnosis is probably insufficient. Either ask your partner **Ask** or a close friend to help you with your diagnosis, or you could take **someone for** your problems to a qualified practitioner. **help**

■ **If you have chosen more than seven flowers**
In earlier literature the number of flowers per mixture was given as between three and six. However, experience today has shown that

because of often massively disrupted emotional balance, the first mixture taken may meaningfully contain up to twelve flower remedies.

Treat any acute state first

● If you have to reduce the number of flower remedies, concentrate first of all on your acute, i.e. immediate, negative emotional symptoms which, as a rule, will be less than six. Then supplement your choice with two or three flower remedies more appropriate to your "chronic", i.e. long-term, state of mind.

● Flower remedies which are particularly appropriate for acute conditions are: Elm, Gorse, Hornbeam, Olive, Rock Rose, Sweet Chestnut, White Chestnut.

Complementary flower remedies

Experience has shown that various negative emotional symptoms tend to occur simultaneously, for example:

Emotional symptoms that complement each other

● Fear of examinations and feelings of inferiority
● Impatience and intolerance
● Despair and guilt

These emotional symptoms can occur side by side with equal intensity, or one of them can cause the other. In either case it is a good idea to take the appropriate flower remedies for both in a single mixture since they will complement each other.

Consideration of a complementary flower remedy is recommended particularly when you are able to find only one or two flowers to suit you. If you have selected several flower remedies the chances are that the appropriate "complementary flower" will be among them.

You will find indications about complementary flowers included in the detailed descriptions which start on page 39. These indications are merely suggestions and do not claim to provide a complete list. Find out whether the flower indicated suits your situation. It is always possible that none of them will strike a chord for you. In this case just stay with the flowers you originally chose.

The repertory

Emotional Symptom	Description	Flower
Absent-minded	*see also* concentrate; forgetful	Clematis, Honeysuckle, White Chestnut
Acceptance	– unable to accept self – unable to accept others – unable to accept one's fate	Larch Beech Vine, Willow
Accident	– consequences of	Star of Bethlehem
Acquiescent	*see* compliant	
Affected	– appears affected	Agrimony
Aggressive		Holly
Aimless		Wild Oat
Alone	– do not want to be alone – want to be alone	Agrimony, Chicory, Heather Clematis, Impatiens, Water Violet
Ambitious	– over-ambitious – lack ambition	Rock Water, Vervain, Vine Clematis, Wild Rose
Angry	– get angry quickly	Holly
Appalled	*see* horrified	
Appreciation	– desire for appreciation	Larch
Arrogant	– give this impression because of shyness – consider others incompetent	Water Violet Beech, Rock Water Vine
Assertive	find it hard to be assertive because of: – lack of faith in own opinion – fear of conflict – lack of self-confidence – fear of offending others – inability to say "No"	 Cerato Agrimony Larch Centaury Centaury

Emotional Symptom	Description	Flower
Attention	– desires attention	Chicory, Heather
Authoritarian	– try to dominate others	Vine
Autocratic	*see* domineering	
Bad conscience	– often have a bad conscience	Pine
Bad luck	– feel dogged by bad luck	Willow
Blocked	– feel blocked	Star of Bethlehem
Blushing	– blush easily	Mimulus, Larch
Bossy	*see* domineering	
Broody	– tend to brood on things	Honeysuckle
Cajole	*see* persuade	
Calm	– lack of calmness	Beech, Impatiens, Mimulus, Rock Water, Vervain
Care, worry	– do not care sufficiently, *see* irresponsible – worry about relatives – feel overwhelmed by worry	Red Chestnut Agrimony
Changeable	*see* unstable	
Clumsy	– in thought and action	Cerato, Chicory, Crab Apple
Company	– feel a need for company, *see* alone	
Compliant	– from fear of conflict – cannot say "No" *see also* yielding	Agrimony Centaury
Conceited		Chicory, Heather, Vine
Concentrate	cannot concentrate because – of inattention – thoughts run ahead – of brooding on the past – thoughts circle around one subject	Chestnut Bud Clematis Honeysuckle White Chestnut

Concentrate (Continued)	– thoughts dart about – every distraction is welcome	Scleranthus Agrimony
Conflict	– fear of	Agrimony, Centaury
Conscientious	– over-conscientious	Crab Apple, Pine, Rock Water
Constant mental activity	– cannot switch off	White Chestnut, Vervain
Control	*see* Thrall	
Critical	– of others – of self	Beech, Chicory Vine, Larch, Pine Rock Water
Criticism	– cannot tolerate	Chicory, Larch, Pine
Cruel	– to people and animals	Holly, Vine
Decision	cannot easily take decisions – but seek no advice – but seek advice – when emotional detachment is needed	 Scleranthus Cerato Walnut
Defiant		Holly
Dejected	*see* melancholy	
Depressed	– by difficulties and setbacks – for no apparent reason – by failure to fulfil one's expectations – life appears meaningless – everything seems hopeless, *see* hopeless – unable to reach a decision – through embitterment – through feelings of inferiority – through inability to overcome negative or sad memories	Gentian Mustard, Wild Rose Pine Wild Oat Scleranthus Willow Larch Honeysuckle, Star of Bethlehem
Despairing		Elm, Larch, Pine Sweet Chestnut

Emotional Symptom	Description	Flower
Despondent	– easily become despondent	Clematis Wild Rose Wild Oat
Difficulty	– always have same difficulties – easily discouraged by difficulties – do not give up in the face of	Chestnut Bud Gentian Oak
Direction	– loss of	Scleranthus, Wild Oat
Dirtied	– feel dirtied, tainted *see also* soiled	Crab Apple
Disadvantaged	– constantly feel disadvantaged	Willow, Chicory
Disappointed	– at lack of expected thanks – expected more from life	Chicory Willow
Discouraged easily	– in the face of difficulty – by anything new	Elm, Gentian, Willow Larch
Disgust	– at dirt, sweat	Crab Apple
Disheartened	– lose heart quickly	Gentian, Larch Wild Oat
Disinclination	– feel weak and lacking in drive	Hornbeam, Larch Mustard, Olive Wild Rose
Dispirited	*see* disheartened	
Dissatisfied	– with oneself	Beech, Chicory Willow
Distraction	– feel need for distraction	Agrimony
Divided	– feel inwardly divided	Centaury, Cherry Plum, Scleranthus
Dogmatic		Vine
Domineering		Chicory, Vine
Doubt	– doubt in oneself – doubts in own opinion	Larch, Pine Cerato

Doubt (Continued)	– doubt about the future	Gentian
	– doubt about ability to cope with work	Hornbeam
	– doubt about ability to continue shouldering responsibility	Elm
	– doubt the ability of others	Beech, Impatiens Vine
Drive	– lacking in drive, feel weak	Hornbeam, Larch Mustard, Olive Wild Rose
Egoistic		Chicory, Heather Willow
Embittered		Holly, Willow
Enraged	*see* furious	
Envy		Holly, Willow
Equanimity	lack of, *see* calm	
Erratic		Scleranthus
Exaggerates	– make mountains of molehills	Crab Apple
Excited	– easily excitable	Beech, Holly Impatiens
Exhausted	– by long illness or stress	Olive
	– by everyday routine	Hornbeam
	– through lack of relaxation	Vervain
	– through overtaxing strength	Centaury, Oak Vervain
	– by always seeking perfection	Rock Water, Pine
	– because a job has to be done	Elm
	– too willing and good-natured	Centaury
	– exceeded limits of strength	Oak
	– due to over-commitment	Vervain
	– expects too much of oneself	Pine, Rock Water
Experience	– tend not to learn from	Chestnut Bud
Exploited	– easily exploited	Centaury
	– feel exploited	Chicory

Emotional Symptom	Description	Flower
Failure	– feel a failure	Pine
	– fear of failure	Elm, Hornbeam
		Larch, Oak
Faith	have little faith, *see* doubt	
Fanatical		Rock Water, Vervain
Fear	– of concrete things or situations	Mimulus
	– of hurting others	Centaury
	– of damaging others or oneself	Cherry Plum
	– of rejection	Centaury, Larch
	– of contagion	Crab Apple
	– of ridicule	Larch
	– of noise	Mimulus
	– of failure	Larch, Mimulus
	– of unexplainable things	Aspen
	– of losing self-control	Cherry Plum
	– of not succeeding	Larch
	– of vague, shadowy things	Aspen
	– of everything	Mimulus
	– of going mad	Cherry Plum
	– panic fears, fear of death	Rock Rose
	– in threatening situations	Rock Rose
	– for others	Red Chestnut
	– of arguments, quarrels	Agrimony
	– of losing control	Aspen
Fickle	*see* unreliable	
Fixed ideas	– in views and behaviour	Beech, Oak
		Rock Water
		Vervain, Vine
Foreboding	– of threatening misfortune	Aspen
Forgetful		Chestnut Bud
Frustrated	– easily frustrated	Holly, Impatiens
		Wild Oat,
Furious	– easily infuriated	Holly

Give up	– find it hard to give up or give in	Oak
	– tend to give up easily	Gentian, Larch
		Wild Oat, Wild Rose
Gloomy	*see* melancholy	
Good-natured	– allows oneself to be exploited	Centaury
Guilt	– blame oneself	Pine
	– blame others	Willow
Harmony, need for	– unwilling to upset others	Centaury
	– feel physically ill during quarrels	Agrimony
Hate, feelings of	– arise quickly	Holly, Willow
Headstrong	*see* obstinate	
Helpful	– cannot refuse anyone	Centaury
	– feel responsible for others	Oak
	– but await gratitude	Chicory
Helpless	– do not know what to do	Cerato, Scleranthus
		Wild Oat
	– afraid of doing the wrong thing	Larch
	see also assertive	
Hesitant		Cerato, Gentian
Homesick		Honeysuckle
Hopeless	– feel hopeless	Agrimony, Gorse, Oak, Pine, Sweet Chestnut, Wild Rose
Horrified	– easily horrified	Rock Rose
Hot-tempered	– prone to violent rages	Cherry Plum, Holly
Hypersensitive	*see* over-sensitive	
Ignored	– feel ignored	Chicory, Willow
Impatient	– when things go too slowly	Impatiens
	– when others don't pay attention	Vine, Chicory
	– when others fail to be persuaded	Vervain
Impractical	– all fingers and thumbs	Clematis

Emotional Symptom	Description	Flower
Impulsive	– act too impulsively	Impatiens, Vervain
Incapable	– feel incapable/incompetent	Larch, Pine Star of Bethlehem
Inconsistent		Chestnut Bud Scleranthus
Indecisive	– finds it hard to take decisions	Cerato, Gentian, Larch, Scleranthus Wild Oat
Indifferent	to people and situations	
	– due to inner resignation	Wild Rose
	– due to loss of hope	Gorse
	– due to depression *see* depressed	
	– due to exhaustion	Olive
	– because thoughts are on the future	Clematis
	– because thoughts are on the past	Honeysuckle
	– through embitterment	Willow
	– through self-absorption	Heather
Inferiority	– feelings of	Elm, Larch, Pine
Inflexible	*see* fixed ideas	
Influence	– tend to influence others	Chicory, Vervain
Influenceable	– find it hard to say "No"	Centaury
	– when trying to pursue own ideals	Walnut
	– through mistrusting own opinon	Cerato Scleranthus
	– through doubting own ability	Larch
	– when grateful for any distraction	Agrimony
Inhibited	– in dealing with others	Larch, Mimulus Water Violet
Insistent	– demanding, pushy	Heather
Insomnia	*see* sleeplessness	
Insulted	– feel insulted, offended	Chicory

Insupportable	– cannot tolerate oneself	**Larch**
Interest	lack of interest, *see* indifferent	
Intolerant	– intolerant of others	**Beech, Impatiens** **Vervain, Vine**
Irresponsible		**Chestnut Bud**
Irritable	– easily irritated – because others disagree – because things go too slowly – at stupidity of others	**Holly, Impatiens** **Vine, Vervain** **Impatiens** **Beech**
Isolated	– easily feels isolated	**Heather, Impatiens** **Water Violet**
Jealousy		**Holly**
Joy	– lack of joy in life	**Mustard, RockWater** **Rock Rose, Pine**
Learning	– have difficulty in learning	**Chestnut Bud**
Letting go	cannot let go – of memories – of certain ideas – of family and friends	**Honeysuckle** **White Chestnut** **Chicory**
Limelight	– constantly seeking attention	**Chicory, Heather**
Listen	– inability to listen to others	**Heather**
Listless	*see* indifferent	
Lonely	– feel lonely	**Chicory, Heather** **Impatiens** **Water Violet**
Loss	– cannot overcome loss – is the cause of suffering	**Honeysuckle** **Star of Bethlehem**
Lost	– feel lost	**Gorse** **Sweet Chestnut**
Madness	– fear of losing one's mind	**Cherry Plum**
Malicious		**Holly**

Emotional Symptom	Description	Flower
Manipulative	*see* influence	
Melancholy		Gentian, Mustard Honeysuckle, Willow
Memory	– have poor memory	Clematis Chestnut Bud
Mental breakdown	– fear of mental breakdown	Cherry Plum
Minimize	– make light of problems to others – minimize own achievements	Agrimony Larch
Minor things	– sensitive about minor things	Crab Apple, Beech
Miserable	– feel miserable	Clematis, Larch Aspen, Mimulus
Mistrust		Gentian, Holly Willow
Misunderstood	– feel misunderstood	Chicory, Heather Willow
Monday-morning feeling	*see* sluggish	
Moody		Holly, Scleranthus
Negative attitude	– towards self – towards others – on principle – temporary	Larch Beech, Willow Gentian Holly
Neglected	– feel neglected	Chicory, Heather
Nervous		Agrimony Impatiens, Oak Mimulus, Vervain
Nervous breakdown	– fears of imminent	Cherry Plum Oak, Vervain
Nightmares		Aspen, Rock Rose
Obstinate		Chicory, Rock Water Vine, Vervain

Obstructed	*see* blocked	
Offended	easily offended	
	– by lack of gratitude in others	Chicory
	– through feeling ignored	Chicory, Willow
Openness	– lack openness towards others	Agrimony
		Water Violet
Over-caring	– for the welfare of others	Chicory
		Red Chestnut
	– mainly for one's own welfare	Heather
		Rock Water
	– about minor matters	Crab Apple
Over-sensitive	– can "hear the grass growing"	Aspen
	see also sensitive	
Overtaxed	– feel overtaxed	Elm, Hornbeam
	see also exhausted	Larch, Oak, Olive
Overworked	– take on too much	Oak, Rock Water
		Vervain
	– feel overworked, *see* exhausted	
Panic	– prone to panic attacks	Aspen, Rock Rose
Perfectionist	– everything must be perfect	Beech, Crab Apple
		Rock Water, Vervain
Perplexed	*see* helpless	
Perseverance	– have too little perseverance	Gentian, Scleranthus
		Wild Oat
	– persevere too long	Oak, Rock Water
		Vervain
Persuade	– allow oneself to be persuaded	Centaury, Cerato
		Larch, Scleranthus
	– tries to persuade others	Vervain, Vine
Pessimist	– always have negative expectations	Gentian
Poisoned	feels poisoned, *see* soiled	
Possessive		Chicory

Emotional Symptom	Description	Flower
Power-seeking		Chicory, Vine
Preaching	– try constantly to convince others	Vervain
Proud	– refuse the help of others	Water Violet
	– tend to be proud	Beech, Vine
		Water Violet
Quick-tempered		Holly, Impatiens
Refuse	– find it hard to refuse anything	Centaury
	– denial of self	Crab Apple, Larch
	– refusal of anything unfamiliar	Beech
Rejected	– feel rejected	Chicory
		Willow
Rejection	fear of rejection, *see* fear	
Relax	– find it difficult to relax	Vervain, Rock Water
		Impatiens
Repressed	– feel repressed	Centaury, Larch
		Walnut
	– repress others	Chicory, Vine
Reproachful	– quick to reproach others	Beech, Chicory
		Impatiens, Willow
Resentful		Honeysuckle, Willow
Reserved	– appear reserved	Mimulus
		Water Violet, Larch
Resigned	– have completely given up	Gorse, Wild Rose
Resilient, resistant	no longer feel resilient due to	
	– total exhaustion	Olive, Hornbeam
	– despair	Sweet Chestnut
	– depression, *see* depressed	
Responsible	– feel responsible for everything	Oak
Restless		Impatiens
		Scleranthus

Sad	*see* depressed	
Sceptical		Gentian
Self-blame		Pine, Rock Water
Self-confidence	lack of, *see* inferiority	
Self-pity		Chicory
Self-respect	lack of, *see* inferiority	
Self-righteous		Rock Water, Vine
Self-sacrificing	– sacrifice too much for others	Centaury, Chicory
Sensitive	– to criticism	Centaury, Larch
Shock	– in all shock situations	Star of Bethlehem
Shyness		Larch, Mimulus
Sleeplessness		Agrimony, Pine Scleranthus White Chestnut
Sluggish	– feel mentally sluggish	Hornbeam
Soiled	– feel inwardly and outwardly soiled	Crab Apple
Spiteful		Holly
Stress	– have put oneself under stress	Vervain
Strict	– with oneself – with others	Rock Water Beech, Chicory, Vine
Stubborn	*see* obstinate	
Suicidal	– suffer from suicidal thoughts	Cherry Plum
Superstitious		Aspen
Sympathy	– cannot feel or show sympathy	Vine
Tact	displays little or no tact because of – impatience – outspokenness	 Impatiens Rock Water, Vine
Take things to heart		Gentian, Larch Rock Water

Emotional Symptom	Description	Flower
Talkative	– talk constantly about own concerns – talk too quickly – talk to cover nervousness	Heather Impatiens, Vervain Mimulus
Tense	– feel tense, uptight	Rock Water, Vervain
Tension		Impatiens, Vervain Rock Water, Vine
Tether	end of, *see* exhausted, despairing	
Thoughts	– same thoughts circle round and round – too lazy to think – erratic thoughts – negative thoughts about others – negative thoughts about self – negative thoughts about the future – torturing thoughts when alone – dreamy thoughts – always thinking of the past	White Chestnut Hornbeam Scleranthus Beech, Holly Larch Gentian, Willow Agrimony Clematis Honeysuckle
Thrall	– try to keep control over others	Chicory, Vine
Tired	– often feel tired	Clematis, Oak Hornbeam, Olive Mustard, Pine Vervain, Wild Rose
Tiresome	– tire or bore others with questions	Cerato
Torn	*see* divided	
Tranquillity	lack of, *see* calm	
Trust	*see* doubt	
Tyrannical	*see* domineering	
Unattractive	– see oneself as unattractive – see others as unattractive	Crab Apple, Larch Beech
Unbalanced		Scleranthus
Uncertain	– of making the right decision	Cerato, Scleranthus Walnut

Uncertain (Continued)	– of being able to master a task	Elm, Hornbeam Wild Oat
	– of one's own path in life	Wild Oat
	– if one is doing things right	Larch, Pine
Uncontrolled		Holly
Undecided	– find it hard to make decisions	Cerato, Gentian Larch, Scleranthus Wild Oat
Ungrateful	– find others ungrateful	Chicory
Unhappy	*see* depressed	
Unjust	– feel unjustly treated	Willow
	– treat others unjustly	Beech, Holly, Vine
Unreliable		Scleranthus Wild Oat
Unsociable		Water Violet
Unstable	– appear or feel unstable	Scleranthus
Value	– feel of little value	Larch, Pine
Vengeful		Holly
Vicious		Holly
Volatile	*see* unreliable	
Weak-willed		Centaury, Gentian Larch
Weakness	*see* exhausted	
Weepy		Chicory, Heather
Withdrawn	*see* openness	
Work	– unable to leave work undone	Rock Water
	– difficulty in "getting going"	Crab Apple Hornbeam
Yielding	– too yielding *see also* compliant	Agrimony, Centaury Larch

An A to Z of Bach flower remedies

In this chapter you will find detailed descriptions of the emotional states attributed to each of the 38 remedies.

Take a little time to read through all of the descriptions. If a flower remedy is appropriate in your case, you will clearly recognize your feelings or your behaviour in its description. The paragraph headed "How your life can change for the better" gives suggestions of how you can achieve a more profound life with the help and support of the flower remedies.

Agrimony

*We would gain far more were we to
show ourselves as we are than by trying
to appear what we are not.*
La Rochefoucauld

Do you try to avoid conflict and argument because situations such as these make you feel physically unwell? Do you often put on a cheerful face, even when you are not feeling on top of the world? Are you inclined to make light of your problems and give the impression that all is well? Do you feel happiest in the company of others? Does it upset you if others are aware of your difficulties, weaknesses, irritations and frustrations? Do you suffer from torturing thoughts that you are unable to talk about? If you answer yes to most of these, you are likely to be one of those people whose principles include, "Keep smiling – what goes on inside is nobody's business but my own!" And you probably get on very well using this motto.

However, going through life in this way takes a great deal of strength and often brings inner loneliness. There is no-one who can comfort you in your worry and despair because you will not permit it. Difficulties and weaknesses appear to you as faults which are better concealed from others.

Agrimony

The result of all this is that you are never truly yourself but are always putting on some sort of show. This demands energy and effort which can ultimately lead to tension in both the mental and physical spheres.

The worst thing of all for these people is to be left alone, because then their outer face, the façade they have built for themselves which they show the world, can no longer protect them from their problems and they find themselves face to face with them. They like this as little as the arguments with other people they try so hard to avoid. Distraction is often the chosen way out, either by seeking company or by means of alcohol.

How your life can change for the better

Little by little, the flower essence of Agrimony will help you find the courage to open your heart to others. Try telling someone about your weaknesses and difficulties. You will discover that others do not reject or criticize you because of them. And conversation such as this will be a relief for you and will help you to believe that life without a mask is possible. The energies that you currently used to keep up your "front" will be released and you will be able to use them to build up the strength you need to tolerate conflict with others more easily.

Complementary flowers (page 22): Mimulus, White Chestnut

Aspen

Anxiety knocked at the door,
confidence answered, and there
was no-one there.
Chinese saying

You often have forebodings and feelings of fear

Do you often feel afraid in the dark or when you are alone? Are there times when cold shudders suddenly run down your spine and a nameless fear arises in you? Do you sometimes wake up in the night in a "cold sweat" as if from a nightmare? Do you ever lie rigid in bed with your heart beating like a hammer, waiting to hear steps on the stairs?

If so, you are among those people familiar with "Aspen fear" – an apparently groundless, indescribable fear which, in extreme cases, can be accompanied by outbreaks of perspiration and intense trembling.

Any attempt to talk to other people about such feelings inevitably fails – they tend to make remarks about "overwork" or "imagination". You, on the other hand, have known such fears since childhood, when you were perhaps only able to go to sleep if a light was left on in your room, or you were frightened of "ghoulies and ghosties" and unknown things under the bed.

Aspen

Like the filigree foliage of the Aspen which reacts so sensitively to every breath of wind, you react to signals from your own and other people's subconscious minds. It is difficult for you to "process" the flood of information that comes in. The result is a chaotic muddle which makes it difficult for you to identify the individual messages. Everything that the "receiver" is unable to categorize and process can create feelings of fear in sensitive and emotional people.

■ How your life can change for the better

Increased under- standing of the wider context
Aspen can help you to gain sufficient inner confidence and strength to enable you to react calmly and collectedly to signals. It will then become possible for you to process all the messages you receive and transform them into creative potential. The confidence that Aspen gives can replace the "pseudo-confidence" of occultism and superstition where you might previously have sought refuge from your fears.

Complementary flowers (see page 22): Rock Rose, Mimulus

Beech

Loveless criticism is a sword that seems to maim others but, in reality, cripples only the critic's heart.
Christian Morgenstern

Are you quick to recognize faults and weakness in others? Does it worry you if those around you pay too little attention to their appearance? Do you often watch the lives and activities of others with a critical eye? Are you prone to be one of those critical people who quickly realize all the things that could be improved upon? Then you probably not only have a sharp sense of observation but are also fairly intolerant.

Most of us would find an admission like this difficult, and sometimes we are quite incapable of acknowledging such a reality because of a lack of self-knowledge. In such cases we should accept and carefully test the gentle prods of friends and relations.

You find it difficult to see others' viewpoints

The problem with intolerant people is the fixed opinion they hold of others and their behaviour, whereby they (the intolerant ones) use their own way of behaving and their own opinion as a yardstick. Any deviation from this is unacceptable and leads them to reject or condemn others.

We are all entitled to think that something is good or bad, beautiful or ugly. However, we must learn to accept that other people have different views. For example, some people will consider it essential to wear their Sunday best for a visit to the opera, while others will be happy to go in jeans. It is clear that differences between ourselves and others can perhaps rub us up the wrong way, or even cause us anxiety at a conscious or unconscious level. But it must not lead us to judge others or look down on them simply because their individuality is different from our own. We all have faults and weaknesses, many of which we are unaware of most of the time – or would possibly prefer not to be made aware of.

Beech

■ How your life can change for the better

Dr Bach's Beech flower remedy can sharpen our sense of observation with regard to our own faults and weaknesses. At the same time it helps us to develop tolerance and generosity towards others. Try practising seeing the good things about people: instead of looking for their faults, see if you can find positive characteristics. You will be amazed how many positive things you can discover if you try.

Complementary flowers (see page 22): Vine, Impatiens, Rock Water, Water Violet, Vervain, Willow

Centaury

*A "no" in time saves much
aggravation.*
German proverb

You are afraid of offending others

Are you one of those willing people who find it difficult to refuse a request? Are you well-known for your good-naturedness? Is it difficult for you to say "no", even if it means, for example, that you are going to be pressed for time or are getting yourself into financial difficulties? Perhaps you often feel tired, overtaxed and exploited, but even then it is hard for you to refuse the requests or wishes of others for fear of offending them.

There is often an old "programme" behind all this – one that you learnt during your childhood. It went something like this: "If you don't do what I want then you are naughty and I shan't love you anymore." People with this experience find it hard to refuse others from a subconscious fear of losing their esteem or affection. They are thus easily influenced by others and often find it difficult to live their own lives properly. The weakness of not being able to refuse can ultimately cause these people not to do things that are important for their own personal needs, things that they should do. It can happen that they go off on holiday to a destinations where they feel ill at ease simply because their partner wanted to go there. Or they take on the running of the family firm, in spite of the fact that they would much rather have become ballet dancers or engineers.

Even in everyday life, in less important situations, they find it difficult to assert themselves and stand up for their own opinions. The result is sometimes that they give up considering their own needs and wishes altogether. In the end these needs are not even acknowledged because Centaury people feel, subconsciously, that they lack the necessary strength to stand up for them. No wonder that much joy in life often gets lost along the way.

■ How your life can change for the better

The Centaury flower essence can support you in developing your ability to say "no". Practise at first on the less important things, like when you go shopping. When the sales person asks if there is anything else you require try saying "no" without hesitation. The next time a friend rings up and wants to take you somewhere you have no desire to go, simply say: "no, I don't really want to, thank you. Perhaps some other time."

You will be surprised to find that nobody really minds when you say no and stick to your own opinion. On the contrary, you will find that people respect you all the more. Only when you learn to say no at the right time will you be able to live your life according to your own wishes and needs, irrespective of the opinions of other people.

Complementary flowers (see page 22): Larch, Cerato, Mimulus, Star of Bethlehem, Chestnut Bud, Honeysuckle

Cerato

Counsel in human hearts is like
water deep down: the understanding
one draws it up.
Jewish saying

Do you often ask other people's advice? Are you often uncertain about decisions and then carry out private opinion polls by asking such questions as "What would you do in my place?" Are you easily influenced by the opinions of others only to discover later on that your own would have been the right one after all? You are thinking, for example, of buying a pair of trousers and you spontaneously choose blue ones; but on the advice of the sales person you buy green ones. Back home you stand in front of the mirror disappointed because the blue trousers would have suited you better – and you knew this at the time.

When uncertain you ask advice of others

Cerato

This happens to you in many situations. You make a spontaneous decision but have no faith in it. You possess lots of intuition to enable you to make the right decisions, but you lack the confidence to trust your inner convictions. You are repeatedly irritated by your "wrong" decisions and become progressively more uncertain; but you never find the courage to trust your own ideas and to work purposefully towards their realization.

■ **How your life can change for the better**
This is a situation where Dr Bach's Cerato flower remedy can help. Take heart and give your intuition a chance. Cerato will support you. From one decision to the next you will become more and more courageous – and you will be surprised what good advice your inner voice gives you.

Complementary flowers (see page 22): Mimulus, Chestnut Bud, Larch, Star of Bethlehem

Cherry Plum

Every crisis holds not only its dangers but also its opportunities.
Martin Luther King

Are you sometimes frightened by your own outbursts of feeling? Are you prone to violent and uncontrolled **You are** outbursts of temper which sometimes shock even you? **prone to** Do you sometimes fear you will lose control of your feelings **violent** and do yourself or someone else damage? Perhaps you feel **rages** rather like a pressure cooker in which the pressure has risen to such an extent that it could explode at any moment. Or you might even feel that a nervous breakdown is imminent.

In this case you are among those people who had to learn in infancy to repress their feelings. How often have we observed children who have had their bubbling high spirits

Cherry Plum

"trained" out of them because, for example, of a necessity to consider neighbours who are sensitive to noise. Particularly in the case of highly emotional people, these repressive mechanisms can lead to a massive repression of feelings. But feelings must be expressed and experienced. The result is that you feel the inner pressure and are afraid that the repressed feelings might one day break out violently – like the waters in a reservoir where the dam can no longer resist the pressure behind it. This is the reason for your fear: that one day you will completely let rip, putting all control mechanisms out of action.

■ How your life can change for the better

Cherry Plum will help you learn gradually to reduce the inculcated blockades and to give your feelings the room they need from moment to moment; this also includes the sexual sphere. This does not mean that you will become an uncontrolled being but rather that a degree of balance can be introduced between the "holding on" or the controlling and the "letting go" of feelings, precisely as you feel is right for you.

I can "live" with my feelings

Complementary flowers (see page 22): Star of Bethlehem, Honeysuckle

Chestnut Bud

He who has a poor memory will always repeat his mistakes.
Indian saying

Are you one of those people who regularly feel under pressure as soon as they have to face a deadline? Even if you have plenty of time at first, you always end up with too little. Something constantly crops up to delay you – a telephone call, a visiting neighbour, a colleague, or something that suddenly has to be dealt with. Do you often spend your holidays in the same place in spite of the fact that you complain about it every time and swear

Bud of the Red Chestnut

Many situations are repeated in your life you will never go there again? Do you find it difficult to remember things? Are you constantly finding yourself in similar situations which you really intended to avoid?

For the onlooker it appears as if you never learn from negative experience or errors made, that you never seem to draw the obvious conclusions. Perhaps this is because you live in the world of your own thoughts and fail to pay sufficient attention to your own, real behaviour; this then plays tricks on you and allows you repeatedly to make the same mistakes. Or perhaps you grasp all the connections but quickly forget your negative experiences and in this way become a "repeat offender". On the one hand, it is good that we should be able to let go of old experiences and forget them. On the other, however, we learn from our mistakes only when we recognize them as such and integrate their consequences into our subsequent actions; that is to say, we adapt our behaviour according to our experience.

■ **How your life can change for the better**
Experience has shown that situations reappear in our lives until we have learned the necessary lesson. We are repeatedly confronted with the same problems until we are prepared to draw the conclusions that are necessary for our development.

Chestnut Bud can help to sharpen your attention to your behaviour. You will be more clearly aware of the world about you, you will "learn your lessons" better and be more easily able to exploit them to your best advantage.

Chicory

Experience shows us that love does not consist in gazing at each other but in looking together in the same direction.
Antoine de Saint-Exupéry

Are you constantly doing things for your family? Do you suffer because your children take too little notice of you? Do you often feel that your commitment to the welfare of the family or other people is too little appreciated? Do you sometimes feel unloved and exploited by everyone?

If so, you share the fate of many people, above all parents, who are prepared to sacrifice themselves totally. In so doing, however, you have definite ideas about good and evil, in accordance with which you seek to guide and shape your family and other people. If your well-intentioned advice proves unwelcome, you feel disappointed, frustrated and unhappy. On top of all this, you have the feeling that people are taking advantage of you. In your opinion, you receive far too little appreciation and affection for all the trouble you take on behalf of others. And love and attention are very important to you. If you could have your way, you would always be with your family.

You wait in vain for the gratitude of others

However, what you regard as a natural motherly or fatherly instinct, namely the exertion of influence in the best interests of your children, is often felt by those children as restrictive and burdensome. And that is when things start getting problematical. For many parents try, quite unconsciously, to weave an emotional network whose warp and weft consist of gratitude and moral obligation.

In his book *Heal Thyself* (Chapter V), Dr Bach writes: "Parenthood is a sacred duty, temporary in its character and passing from generation to generation. It carries with it nothing but service and calls for no obligation in return from the young, since they must be left free to develop in their own way and become as fitted as possible to fulfil the same office in but a few years' time." In other words, when parents render their children services they should expect no thanks in return. When parents slave voluntarily for their children, this is done at their own wish and often goes against the desires of the children. Why, then, should children feel any gratitude? The often-heard lament of parents, "Look at all I've done for my children and that's all the thanks I get!" arises from a misunderstanding. If I want to give something to somebody there must be no expectation of receiving anything in return, otherwise my gift is not a gift at all, it is a commercial investment.

Chicory

Another misunderstanding, widespread not only among parents, is the claim of wanting to do the best for the other, be it partner or child. How are we to know what is best for someone else? It will always be "our best", namely as seen from our standpoint and therefore subjectively coloured and often miles away from what is really best for the other. These thoughts might lead you to reflect and even to discover, perhaps through discussion with your children, how you behave towards them.

■ How your life can change for the better
The flower essence of Chicory can support you in building a different, perhaps more selfless, parent–child relationship. This

Unselfish love leaves others room to move

includes letting go of the children Chicory will give you the strength to learn to accept that children have to go their own way, even if this does not accord with our wishes and way of seeing things. Have faith in your children – that is the surest talisman you can give them on their way.

Complementary flowers (see page 22): Red Chestnut, Vine

Clematis

That which we do today decides how
the world looks tomorrow.
Marie von Ebner-Eschenbach

Are you always building castles in the air? Do you often imagine situations in which all is well with you and your problems vanish like the morning dew? Do you spend a lot of time dreaming about winning the lottery or being lucky in love? Are you easily prone to take refuge from cold, grey everyday life in a colourful world of fantasy and illusion?

Dreaming with our eyes open does us all good and is even recommended as balm for the troubled soul. However, in some people this sort of daydreaming can become the main content of their lives and serves as a defence mechanism against all the difficulties that can arise in day-to-day living. Instead of seeking

You take
refuge from
everyday life
in a dream
world

a concrete solution in the present, these people flee with their thoughts into a future that holds no more problems for them.

In reality, of course, their problems remain unsolved because they seek no down-to-earth solution for them. This usually leads to renewed difficulties, which are again intensified by flight into an imaginary world. These people run the risk of distancing themselves more and more from the present and of losing all interest in it. They give those around them the impression of lacking concentration, of being apathetic and disinterested. When they are ill, for example, they do not seem to care whether or how quickly they return to health. Moreover, the danger of seeking refuge in alcohol or other drugs cannot be excluded in this form of "overcoming problems".

■ How your life can change for the better

In extreme cases, Clematis can provide support during psychiatric therapy aimed at reawakening the ability to solve problems in the here and now.

In addition to this serious and long-lasting form of the Clematis state, there is a less pronounced form that can occur in any of us at any time. This is when our thought processess are impaired by intense happiness or extreme aggravation, guilt or jealousy. At such times our thoughts can dash off to future events (if they turn to the past, see Honeysuckle), and we become inattentive and lack concentration. Or we daydream at the most inopportune times, such as at work, at school or when driving. We fail to recognize old friends coming towards us in the street, we forget to get off the bus, or we overlook the red light at the crossroads. In these situations, too, Clematis can quickly help us to regain control of our thoughts.

Complementary flower (see page 22): White Chestnut

Clematis

Crab Apple

*Life creates order but order does not
give rise to life.*
Antoine de Saint-Exupéry

Can a stain on your blouse or the tablecloth upset
you? Is cleanliness and order necessary for your
well-being, above all when you are on holiday or in
hot climates? Is attention to your appearance
such that a spot on your face can make you
downright unhappy? Do you feel unclean if
you are unable to take a shower immediately
after any strenuous activity? Do you pay too much
attention to unimportant details at the expense
of the overall view? Are your thoughts often
blocked by minor details? Then you are perhaps
one of those people who get too caught up in
trivialities, who find it difficult to get their
priorities right and to recognize what is
important and what is not.

Crab Apple

    The Crab Apple flower remedy can help you
to develop a feeling for right relations and proportions, to learn to
differentiate between the important and the minor. This applies
to all the situations that constantly confront us in everyday life

**Cleanliness
and order
are very
important to
you**

and therefore also to matters of cleanliness and order.
    Some people almost develop a mania in their desire to have
everything absolutely clean and tidy and feel physically and
emotionally uncomfortable if this is not the case. Behind all this
there is often a serious emotional problem manifesting itself in the
form of an extreme desire for cleanliness. Such feelings as those of
being outwardly and inwardly soiled, for example by optical
impressions, conversation, sexual contact, food or clothing, can
also be of a neurotic nature. This is not to be confused with
justified feelings of uncleanliness caused by the environment,
about which people who are perfectly healthy emotionally are
complaining more and more today.

■ **How your life can change for the better**

Dr Bach's Crab Apple remedy – the cleansing flower, as it is sometimes called – can certainly help you. It can free you from your feelings of uncleanliness and bring your attitude towards cleanliness and order into proportion.

You need not fear that Crab Apple will turn you into a sloppy and disorderly person; it will merely lift your sights to more important things, helping you to differentiate between what is important and what is not, and set more appropriate priorities.

Setting other priorities

When, for example, your children come home with wet and dirty shoes, you will be able to pay less attention to the dirty shoes and more to the fact that wet shoes lead to cold feet and possible illness if you fail to take the necessary rapid action.

If someone suffers from a real psychosis in this context, psychiatric therapy is possibly necessary. In this case, Crab Apple can provide helpful support.

Complementary flowers (see page 22): Rock Water, Beech.

Elm

Courage consists not in ignoring danger, but in overcoming it while looking it straight in the eye
Jean Paul

Are you feeling like an experienced high-diver who is standing on the springboard and suddenly feels he cannot dive any more? Do you suddenly feel overwhelmed by the load of work and the responsibility you have to bear? Are you suddenly without courage because you believe that your efforts are in vain and that, in any case, you will have no success?

Perhaps you are familiar with the state of no longer knowing anything or not being capable of anything at all. Normally you are perfectly able to keep on top of things. You have all the advantages of intuition, intelligence and perseverance and are able to do all that is required of you. You enjoy your work and you do it very

You suddenly doubt your own abilities

well. But suddenly, out of a clear blue sky – usually in connection with some new task – you begin to doubt your abilities and you lose courage. You feel weak and exhausted and have the terrible feeling that you are unable to do another thing. For fear of failing you really do make mistakes and end up in a state of total discouragement and depair.

Elm

■ **How your life can change for the better**
This state is usually temporary and does not last long. The flower remedy Elm, however, can help to end it more quickly. You will find your way back to self-confidence and inner security and will once again be capable of performing the tasks required of you. Your confidence in being able to master new tasks will also grow.

Complementary flowers (see page 22):
Gentian, Olive

Gentian

*Mistrust is a two-edged sword which
can hinder more than it protects.*
Lord Byron

Are you easily discouraged when unexpected difficulties arise? For example, you have set a definite date for a cycle tour with friends. A few days before your departure something goes wrong with your bicycle and it has to be repaired. Is your first thought that it won't be ready in time anyway since the damage must surely take longer to be put right? When you are waiting in a queue at the cinema are you sure the last ticket will be sold before you get to the box office? Do you tend to feel depressed if something in your life fails to go as you expected? Are you prone to expect the worst to ensure that you are not disappointed?

If you recognize yourself in these descriptions, you are probably one of a large group of people who go through life with a **You are easily discouraged and are prone to pessimism** pessimistic attitude. You are mostly in a melancholic or depressive frame of mind and cannot believe that you might just once be lucky in life. In accordance with this attitude you tend to see everything in a negative light. The result of this can be that you register only those events which confirm your negative and sceptical expectations. For example, you notice only those days when you wait in the "wrong" queue at the supermarket and it takes ages to get through. You never notice the other days when you wait at the "right" check-out and speed through quickly.

This example can be extended to all the other spheres of your life. Pessimists prove to themselves that they really do usually have bad lack by this sort of "selective perception". They are unhappy when something goes wrong and are unable to recognize that even situations that go awry can have a positive aspect. It is as if they are always wearing dark glasses which allow no positive pictures to filter through.

■ **How your life can change for the better**
If you would like to step out of your "negative programme", you should take the Gentian flower remedy, even if, as a convinced pessimist, you will probably not expect it to help you.

Gentian will emphasize the positive aspect of your perception of all the pleasant things which also happen in your life. You will be able to take off the "dark glasses" through which you have thus far observed everything. Pessimists should also devote some attention to instruction about positive thinking – to a certain extent, optimism can be learned.

Gentian

In addition to the "chronic state of pessimism" there are real situations in which we feel dispirited and discouraged, such as periods of sickness, examinations, or separations. Gentian can help us to face such situations with courage and optimism.

Complementary flowers (see page 22): Larch, Mimulus, Willow

Gorse

*Faith is the bird that sings
when it is still night.*
Tagore

Are you feeling hopeless and discouraged because all your plans have gone wrong? Are you very ill and have you given up hope that there is anything that can help you? Are you in the middle of a personal crisis and cannot believe that things could still turn out to your advantage? Do you feel there is no point in having another go at changing your situation?

Then you are probably in a state of deep resignation. If you do take some steps towards changing your situation you do this not of your own volition but at the prompting of friends and relations. You have resigned yourself totally to your fate. "I cannot change anything; I'll just have to live with it", is the sort of sentiment people will frequently hear you saying, or which you will think to yourself.

Your situation seems hopeless   At first glance such acceptance might appear the enlightened action of the wise person who accepts his or her fate without argument But closer inspection reveals a different picture. It transpires that it is not enlightenment but hopelessness that is leading to such resignation, for satisfaction and joy in living are absent. This is the onset of an inner dying and the need for treatment is therefore urgent.

■ **How your life can change for the better**
Despite the feeling that there is no point to anything anymore, you should take Dr Bach's Gorse flower remedy. It can fan back to life the spark of hope that is dying within you. Perhaps you will then be able to take a new look at your situation and so discover a way out of your difficulties.

Gorse

Heather

*He who overcomes his egoism rids
himself of the most significant obstacle
blocking the path to all true greatness
and all true happiness.*
Tagore

Is it difficult for you to be alone? Do you always need someone
with whom you can discuss yourself and your problems? Is it
important that you are appreciated and noticed by others?
Is it for this reason that you talk so often about your own
You often achievements and your merits? Have you sometimes the feeling
feel too little that others do not listen to you carefully enough? Does it
noticed sometimes happen that friends break off contact in a way you
cannot explain? Do you often have too little time to devote to
other people?

Heather

You are probably among those people who demand the total
attention of others but who are poor listeners themselves.
They are generally so taken up with themselves that they have
too little time, interest and understanding for the concerns of
others. It is generally very difficult for us to recognize and admit
to this sort of behaviour in ourselves. Other people draw our
attention to our egoistic behaviour only very rarely; they are
much more likely to simply withdraw from our company.
While we notice this, it would not occur to us that it had
anything to do with our own egocentricity and we
therefore attribute the fault to others.

Behaviour such as this is, in fact, an S.O.S. for attention
and appreciation. Like small children, we want to be the
centre of attraction in order to concentrate people's minds
on our needs. We are still "fixed" on our own person and
do not have a well-developed feeling for the needs of others.
To this extent our egoistic behaviour means that we got
stuck somewhere along the way in our development from
child to adult.

■ How your life can change for the better

Dr Bach's Heather flower remedy can support you in completing this missing step in your development from child to adult. It will help you to recognize and lay aside your selfish, childishly demanding behaviour. At the same time it will assist in developing your sensitivity to the needs of others, and your ability to take an interest in other people and their affairs will grow accordingly. Your "reward" for this will be that you will experience more attention and appreciation from other people – the very thing that you crave in the first place.

You develop a sensitivity towards others

Even in the lives of people who normally pay attention to others and are good listeners there are times when their own problems force them into a state where they would like best of all to talk non-stop about themselves and their difficulties. In cases such as these Heather can also help. Your inner balance will be quickly restored and you will find your way back to your customary behaviour.

Complementary flowers (see page 22): Chicory, Willow

Holly

When I hate, I detract from myself;
When I love, I am enriched to the
extent of my loving
Friedrich Schiller

Are you prone to lose your temper easily and are you often unfriendly towards those around you? Are you easily irritated and displeased? Would you sometimes like best to smash everything in grabbing distance? Are there times when you get out of bed on the wrong side and are then unfair and unbearable all day long? Does every little thing annoy you? Do you sometimes literally explode from jealousy or envy?

We all know negative feelings and states of mind such as these, even if in varying degrees. Some of us, for example, are merely unfriendly to those around us while others can become violent in their aggressiveness. In some people jealousy manifests itself in constant digs and spiteful remarks while others turn into raging Othellos.

These feelings, be they very marked or less strongly developed, all have something in common: when they are aroused, love and affection fly out of the window. Unloving states such as these can last for varying lengths of time – a few minutes, hours, days, or a whole lifetime.

You are easily irritated and aggressive
In the loss of love Dr Bach sees the cause of all negative feelings such as hate, envy, ill will, jealousy and aggressiveness. These are the triggers of all the evil, cruelty and pain that is constantly happening in the world.

Holly

■ **How your life can change for the better**
With the help of the Holly flower remedy we can learn to recognize and let go of our negative feelings. In this way room is made in us for love and we shall be enabled to behave affectionately towards those around us.

Complementary flowers (see page 22): Impatiens, Willow

Honeysuckle

Life can be understood only in retrospect but it can be lived only by looking forward.
Sören Kierkegaard

Do you often lack concentration because your thoughts wander into the past? Is it difficult for you to forget particularly good or bad times and do you think a lot about them? Do you feel that things were all a lot better in the past than they are today? Or are you unable to escape from the memory of threatening situations? Do you suffer easily from homesickness?

All of us have moments when our thoughts are in the past. It is only when this threatens our relationship with the present, when we are too often inattentive and lacking in concentration, that we have reached a state which requires action for change.

You often think of the past

Hanging on to the past in our thoughts blocks our development in the present. Everything we have experienced in the past has shaped us; on the whole, we have learnt our "lessons" and can let go of the thoughts and memories connected with them. But if, for example, I am constantly yearning for friends that I have "lost" because I have moved to another place, such feelings will block my ability to find new friends. If I am constantly railing against a decision taken, I cannot be open to new decisions.

■ **How your life can change for the better**

Life is like a stairway: it is only when we have left one step that we are able to go on to the next one. It is also only when we can let go of the past that we can begin something new in the present. The Honeysuckle flower remedy can help you to let go of thoughts of the past. Your ability to absorb all that is happening in the present will grow. You will be able to live in the present more attentively and contentedly.

Complementary flowers (see page 22): Pine, White Chestnut, Mimulus, Chestnut Bud, Star of Bethlehem

Honeysuckle

Hornbeam

The human spirit is never more cheerful than when it has found its true vocation.
Wilhelm von Humboldt

Are you one of those people who, on waking, would prefer to pull the blankets over your head at the thought of all you have to get through during the day?

The work lies ahead of you like a vast mountain and you feel too weak to cope with it all. But then the amazing thing happens – by evening you have got through it all beautifully. Hornbeam is also called the "Monday-morning remedy" because this feeling of weakness often comes over us at the beginning of a new week.

Everyday routine wears you out

It happens, above all, when we have to deal with humdrum routine work or less important odd jobs which make more demands on our memories than on our minds. This sort of one-dimensional effort often leads to tiredness and exhaustion which, in turn, takes its toll on the body so that we end up feeling tired and "slack" all over.

Although physical or mental activity would actually do us good, and we know it, we seem unable to make the effort even to go for a walk or visit friends. Instead, we sit in front of the television set watching whatever is on offer, only to awaken the next morning with the same feeling of weakness.

■ How your life can change for the better

The way out of this mental exhaustion will be found more easily with the help of the Hornbeam flower remedy. It will make you mentally more lively and will give you clarity of thought. In order to overcome the paralysing apathy and to help you, if necessary, to counteract a one-dimensional routine in everyday life you could, for example, take an evening class or weekend course, or make an effort to participate in events that would promote mental or physical activity.

Complementary flowers (see page 22): Mustard, Chestnut Bud, Olive.

Hornbeam

Impatiens

Patience is the key to joy.
Arabian proverb

Does it get on your nerves when others speak slowly or are slow in general? Do you find it difficult to stand in a long queue at a supermarket and then have to watch while a customer laboriously fishes each penny out of a purse when paying? Do you find yourself finishing people's sentences for them, or do you even take things out of other people's hands to finish a job yourself because things are going too slowly for you?

Haste and stress only make life difficult for you

If you identify with these descriptions, you are probably one of those impatient people who rush through life at a dizzying speed. You think fast, speak fast and appear nervous and tense, always on the point of either departure or explosion. The company of people who react and act more slowly than you is a great trial of your patience. Because of your ability to grasp things quickly you are prone to feel superior to others, and you become irritated and frustrated if those others are unable to keep up with you.

The problem with impatient people lies both in their dealings with others and with themselves. In dealings with other people everything is measured against their own "fast lane" yardstick. This can easily lead to intolerance and arrogance, and a tendency to consider other people as stupid and incompetent.

However, it has been seen over and over again that precisely because slower people take the time to examine things more thoroughly – that is to say, by dint of their consideration of a matter and their accuracy – they develop a deeper insight into situations than the impatient, quick-witted person who is prone to remain on the surface of things.

In their dealings with themselves, fast-moving, fast-thinking people give themselves little rest. Body and soul find little chance for relaxation: with their thoughts already rushing on ahead, those driven by impatience and restlessness lose the ability to enjoy a

Impatiens

moment's quiet peace and beauty. They find it difficult to sit on a bench in the open air and allow their feet and their souls to dangle. A physical result of all this is that they frequently suffer from cramped muscles and digestive upsets. Unlike the more thoughtful plodding person, the impatient one seldom finds time for deeper contemplation of a matter, or for more in-depth perception into a situation or of other people. As a result they are often over-hasty and superficial in their judgements.

■ How your life can change for the better

Have patience with yourself and others

The Impatiens flower remedy will not slow you down to any great degree. However, it will help you to reduce your hectic restlessness and to become more patient with others and with yourself. Try it and see how pleasant it can be to remain for a while with your thoughts completely in the present. You will see many things with quite different eyes when you lean back in a relaxed way and find inner peace. Perhaps you will also notice that the successes you are constantly chasing are already yours in the here and now.

Complementary flowers (see page 22): Beech, Chestnut Bud

Larch

Lay aside your fears, rely upon your own inner resources, trust in life, and it will repay you. You can do more than you think.
Ralph Waldo Emerson

When you are invited to a party do you find all the other guests seem more interesting and attractive than yourself? Do you feel like a wallflower or a little grey mouse, keeping quiet for fear of saying the wrong thing, only to discover later that what you wanted to say would have been exactly right? In many things that you would like to do, have you the feeling that you are not going to succeed anyway? Are you sensitive to criticism and do you often feel that you are under personal attack? Are you always particularly anxious to hear praise and recognition from others?

Then you are probably one of those people who lack a well-developed sense of their own value. Although you can do just as much and just as well as others – often more and better – you just don't believe you can. For fear of failure or of making yourself look ridiculous, you sometimes never even begin a job or flatly refuse a new task.

You often feel inhibited and dissatisfied with yourself

You usually feel inferior to others right from the start. You are dissatisfied with yourself and your looks and would prefer to be like other people whose talent, appearance or behaviour you very often admire without envy. For you are not an envious person. You lack the ability to accept yourself just as you are. This is called a lack of self-confidence or feeling of inferiority. This underestimation of yourself probably began in early childhood. Perhaps you had a tendency in this direction and grew up in surroundings where your germinating self-confidence wiltedfor lack of nourishment.

But resigning yourself sadly, or attempting to attribute responsibility to a parent who might have got it all wrong, will not help you to advance personally, and neither will it increase your self-confidence.

■ How your life can change for the better
You should begin by doing something about your underdeveloped feelings of self-worth. Try, step by step, to overcome your fear of failure or ridicule. Larch can support you in this, preferably in combination with Mimulus. You will soon feel your self-confidence growing. When you trust yourself to do something you will succeed, and that success will in turn strengthen your sense of self-worth even more.

In addition to this "chronic" state of feeling inferior, there are also acute situations when we feel ourselves lacking in value. A partner leaving us, or not getting a job we wanted, for example, can easily arouse feelings of inferiority, often accompanied by

Larch

resentment or jealousy. In cases such as these Larch can help, preferably in conjunction with Holly or Willow.

Complementary flowers (see page 22): Mimulus, Honeysuckle, Pine, Gentian, Star of Bethlehem, Cerato, Centaury

Mimulus

Joy and fear are magnifying glasses.
Traditional Flemish saying

Certain situations frighten you

Are you one of those people who are frightened every time they go to the dentist, who are scared by thunderstorms or who get butterflies in their insides when an examination looms? Or perhaps you have fears about the future, of becoming old or of sickness. Or you have other fears that you can describe precisely: "I am frightened of . . . "

In this case, you are one of the people for whom Dr Bach discovered the flower Mimulus. The Mimulus fear is typical in that we can definitely describe it (unlike Aspen fears which are inexplicable and vague). Mimulus fears are all concerned with our own person. Either you fear an event that could harm you physically or emotionally, such as a visit to the dentist or separation from a loved one, or you fear failure, for example in a forthcoming examination or making a speech in public.

Whichever aspect of Mimulus fear applies to you, it is ultimately always a question of suffering. Usually, in the past, you have experienced negative situations and fear they might recur. The fact that you tend to expect the negative to happen, rather than looking optimistically towards the future and freeing yourself from past experiences, plays an important role.

Mimulus

■ **How your life can change for the better**
Mimulus can help you to overcome your fears and face up easily and courageously to all challenges. The visit to the

dentist will probably not be transformed into a joyous occasion, and every loss will still bring sorrow and suffering, but you will be better able to cope with these events and, when the time comes, to react in a more measured way.

Complementary flowers (see page 22): Honeysuckle, Star of Bethlehem, Gentian, Larch, Rock Rose.

Mustard

Worry arises from the passing of time that has failed to ripen its fruit.
Antoine de Saint-Exupéry

You feel sad and empty without knowing why

Do you know the feeling of depression and sadness that can unexpectedly overwhelm you like a great black cloud which suddenly hides the sun? You become tired and lacking in drive; you would rather sit miserably in a corner staring at nothing. For no tangible reason you feel sad and low and could burst into tears at the slightest provocation. The world has instantly lost its colour and everything seems meaningless. These feelings usually disappear as fast as they came.

Mustard

If you often suffer from depression like this you are probably one of those people who find it difficult to express anger and, if necessary, to shout and yell. Instead of telling people what is upsetting you, you swallow your rage and then become angry with yourself; that is to say, you ultimately direct against yourself the feelings of aggression which you should be venting. As time goes by your subconscious transforms all this "swallowed" anger into depressive behaviour.

Many women suffer from depression to varying degrees of intensity during the days preceding their periods and during the menopause, which are the times when their hormonal balance is unstable. Quite independently of this physical cause, however, feelings of depression can arise, sometimes as a reaction to a painful experience. Men, too, can be plagued by mood-affecting feelings or suffer from either mild or more serious forms of depression.

■ How your life can change for the better

For all minor cases of depression, Mustard can bring light and colour back into your everyday life. You will feel again a joy in living and vital energy returning. In the case of depression which is a result of a long, physical sickness, Mustard can bring about a noticeable reawakening of your spirits.

Colour returns to your life

Serious depression, which at times can be accompanied by thoughts of suicide, must be treated medically or psychiatrically. However, Mustard can perhaps support treatment such as this, and might even – although only after discussion with the practitioner treating the case – allow for a careful reduction of the prescribed medicines.

Complementary flowers (see page 22): Willow, Gorse, Sweet Chestnut, Larch, Olive

Oak

Endurance is a daughter of strength; obstinacy is a daughter of weakness, namely weakness of the understanding.
Marie von Ebner-Eschenbach

You ought really to be pulling the "emergency brake" because you know that your activities are getting too much for you. You feel tired and without strength, but you wouldn't even consider the possibility of giving up part of your work or organizing help. You just plod on, almost as is you were driven. "Just don't give up", "keep going at any price" might well be your battle cry. "I can't leave the others with all this work" is often your first thought

You would
never dream
of admitting
a weakness

should you fall ill. And your conscientiousness and will to hang on till the bitter end drive you on. Perhaps you fear others might resent your weakness. Perhaps you prefer not to admit that even you have limits. Perhaps you need this "outer" strength in order to feel "inwardly" strong.

■ **How your life can change for the better**
You know the gnarled oak that stands firm in the storm until it suddenly falls? Compare it with the poplar that bends flexibly in the face of the strongest wind. Do you see any similarity between yourself and the oak? Then you should take the Oak flower remedy in order to regain your strength quickly.

In addition, you will develop your ability to recognize and accept your own limits. The will to endure is an important characteristic and many great discoveries would not have been made without it. But, like so many things in life, the main point here is moderation.

Giving up and hanging on are the poles between which the sensible average for yourself lies. The Oak remedy can provide valuable help while you seek it.

Complementary essence (see page 22): Rock Water

Oak

Olive

*It is a lack of understanding
to exceed one's strength.*
Sophocles

Do you know the feeling that you just don't want to do anything at all, not even the things that normally give you pleasure? Is everything too much effort? Do you feel totally wrung out, to such an extent that you would like most of all to go away and hide in a quiet corner? You are unable to contemplate anything productive in the evening and you just hang around or watch some television programme that doesn't really interest you. This

You feel totally exhausted and overtaxed condition indicates total exhaustion. You have probably overtaxed yourself for a long time, ignoring your needs for rest and relaxation.

Are you prone to overlook your own needs out of sheer commitment to a cause or a task? Are you perhaps one of those over-conscientious people who is satisfied only when the job has been done one hundred percent correctly? Or perhaps you are one of the many mothers who sacrifice themselves completely for their families.

These and other similar patterns can result in chronic states of exhaustion due to constant overwork.

■ **How your life can change for the better**
There are two ways of extricating yourself from this unhappy and unacceptable state:

You know the circumstances that have led to your tired and exhausted state. Perhaps these arose from illness, lack of sleep or temporary stress. In this case the Olive flower essence can help to get you back on your feet – only, of course, if you change the situation which is sapping your strength. Olive is not a wonder drug which can magically replace sleep, relaxation or vitamins.

Olive

You are unaware of the causes for your exhaustion. In this case you should first consult a doctor or a healing practitioner to determine whether any organic disturbance might be responsible for your chronic exhaustion. This might include a lack of iron, for example.

If everything is in order in this area, you should pay more attention to your behaviour to discover when and how you are prone to overtaxing your strength. Perhaps you have recognized yourself in the behavioural patterns described above. You should therefore take the Olive flower remedy, together with the complementary remedy best suited to your behaviour in order to treat the root of the trouble. In addition to this, you should try to eliminate the behavioral pattern you have recognized. Olive and "your" complementary flower will help you to do this.

If you have not identified any of the behavioural patterns as being similar to your own, begin by taking the Olive flower remedy then try, in discussion with a trusted friend or an experienced practitioner, to obtain a little more self-knowledge. You will probably then discover the real cause of your exhaustion.

Complementary flowers (see page 22): Centaury, Crab Apple, Larch, Vervain, Rock Water, Chicory, Oak

Pine

It is not my task to give others the objective best, but to keep my own as pure as possible.
Hermann Hesse

Are you often dissatisfied with your achievement because you feel you should have done the job better? Do you always look for the fault in yourself when problems arise with other people? Do you easily suffer from a bad conscience? Do you often feel, for example, that you are not doing justice to the needs of your children or your spouse?

    Then you are probably one of those people who doubt everything that they do and who constantly ask themselves whether they couldn't do everything much better. After a successful birthday dinner party, for example, when all the guests have left, you start asking yourself if perhaps something was not as good as it should have been – had the meal really been enjoyable? had the wine been well chosen? had the atmosphere been comfortable? Such thoughts can actually make you lie awake at night as you torture yourself with reproaches about all the "wrong" decisions you have taken and about all the things you have said which you regret. You even often seek to blame yourself for the mistakes of others.

You often feel you are not doing others justice

Your dissatisfaction and doubt are not restricted to your achievements: they extend to all your human qualities. Even here you find yourself unsatisfactory and inadequate. It doesn't much help either when others insist that the opposite is true. Your feeling of inadequacy sits like a poisoned arrow in your heart. The consequences are uncertainty, a lack of joy in living and the constant effort to do everything particularly well in order to do justice to the high standards you have set yourself. Rather like the "inferiority complex programme" (see Larch), the "guilt programme" also usually commences in childhood.

Pine

■ **How your life can change for the better**
The Pine flower remedy will not free you from your feelings of guilt all at once, but it will bring you strength and assurance to help you try another way of behaving. In everything you do you should try saying: "I will give my very best and if that is not enough for others then that's their problem." Or in other words: "As long as I try to do my best, I have no need to reproach myself, not even when others find me or my achievements inadequate."

Exaggerated feelings of guilt will gradually decrease

In other, temporary situations when we suddenly martyr ourselves with self-reproach, Pine can help us to see both ourselves and the situation in a more balanced light.

Complementary flowers (see page 22): Larch, Honeysuckle, White Chestnut, Rock Water, Crab Apple, Sweet Chestnut, Gorse

Red Chestnut

*Every terrifying vision disappears
when you look it straight in the eye.*
Johann Gottlieb Fichte

Are you unable to go to sleep at night when a son or daughter
has not yet come home? Must your "other half" get in touch
with you frequently when absent from home to calm your fears?
Are you constantly afraid that something could happen to your
child on the way to school? Or, more generally, is frequent or
constant anxiety about those close to you part of your
everyday life?

    If all this sounds like you, you are a classic case for the Red
Chestnut flower. Anxiety for others is the central theme of this
remedy. This anxiety, which at first glance might appear morally
commendable, does not damage only you,: it also affects all
those you worry about so much. For example, a sensitive
child will know when its mother is anxious and will
become insecure.

    Such anxiety, in the final analysis, indicates a lack of
trust – for example, in the child's own abilities. How
can a child in this situation be expected to develop
self-confidence? On the other hand, grown-up
relatives will only feel burdened by the constant
anxieties of others. Anyone who is forced by this
kind of pressure constantly to interrupt their work
or participation in conferences or meetings to
telephone home, irrespective of the inconvenience
involved, knows that the fear of the person at home
is a practical as well as a mental burden.

■ How your life can change for the better
The Red Chestnut remedy can help you to
let go of your fears for others. It will enable you
to think positively about your relations and
loved ones when they are away. Perhaps you will
suddenly realize that the fears which, up till now,

Red
Chestnut

were hidden behind an exaggerated care for the welfare of others were really for fears for yourself. Thus, Red Chestnut can help you not only to overcome your anxieties for others but can also enable you to recognize and master your own fears.

Complementary flowers (page 22): Gentian, Honeysuckle, Star of Bethlehem, Mimulus, Chicory, Rock Rose

Rock Rose

*A victim of shipwreck
fears even calm seas.*
Ovid

During a storm, have you ever been in an aeroplane that suddenly dropped into an air-pocket without warning? Have you ever been in a sailing boat in the middle of a lake during a thunderstorm, aware that the mast was a perfect lightning conductor? Do you know what it feels like to climb out of your car with sagging knees after an accident? Or have you experienced anything similar when you felt you were in mortal danger or entirely at the mercy of a threatening situation? Then you will know the panic that stops the heart, takes one's breath away and leaves one paralyzed from fear.

Rock Rose

We usually become aware of this fear only when the danger has past and the feeling of "being in shock" begins to take hold. It is in this phase that Rock Rose can help to disperse the inner panic, calm the pulse and restore normal breathing. It helps us to awaken from our stricken state and to react in an appropriate way.

For panic attacks and their consequences   Perhaps you are one of those people who, because of a more sensitive nervous system, are overcome by panic in less extreme situations, becoming totally confused and losing sight of the larger picture. Situations such as these can arise when, for example, you suddenly realize you are not going to meet an important deadline, or have lost something precious, or one of the family does not come home on time. In cases such as these, Rock Rose can also help you to react in a more collected manner.

■ How your life can change for the better
You can count on the calming influence of Rock Rose in all crises situations and in the face of all circumstances that personally cause you fear or even terror. See also Rescue Remedy (page 98).

Rock Water

Either one masters life with a smile
or not at all.
Chinese proverb

Does your life run on set rules and principles? Are you in the habit of doing gymnastic exercises or adhering to a diet, for example, with the utmost discipline? Is your work invariably done in an exemplary way? Are you one of those reliable and conscientious workers who are the joy of every employer's heart? Are your expectations of yourself so high that often you are able to come up to them only with great effort?

You will probably now ask, "What's wrong with that? It's not a bad thing to make high demands of oneself and to be disciplined." Of course it is not a bad thing, but only so long as this attitude doesn't cost you your happiness and well-being. Sometimes over-developed conscientiousness and discipline can take on forms that turn us into fanatics and humourless ascetics who lose all joy in living. In this case we are prone to repress those of our needs that do not fit into our ideal picture of ourselves. Our drive for perfection and our adherence to principles sometimes makes us strict, rigid and self-righteous.

You demand too much of yourself

In certain cases, this type of behaviour is not particularly marked and the people concerned perhaps feel only a little lack of lightness and joy.

■ **How your life can change for the better**

The Rock Water remedy is a kind of "softener" that can help you to take yourself a little less seriously and to see the lighter side of life. Even if we don't do everything perfectly and forget our principles from time to time, we are still loveable creatures. You will feel happier and more alive if you make less strict demands on yourself. Try not to be so hard on yourself; you could even spoil yourself rather as a good friend would.

Increase your quality of life through forebearance

Complementary flowers (see page 22): Pine, Crab Apple, Beech, Oak

Rock Water

Scleranthus

When you stand undecided between two things, choose that which seems harder to your baser self, for this finds nothing so arduous as that which is true.
Ibn Atá Alláh

Do you often find it difficult to make a choice between two things? For example, you receive two invitations for the same evening and would like to accept both. What should you do? First one attracts you most, then the other. The longer you think about it, the more arguments for and against you discover and the decision becomes more difficult. In the end your decision making abilities are blocked and perhaps you leave the choice to the toss of a coin. Do you find it difficult to concentrate on a subject or the job in hand because new thoughts are always going through your head? Are you prone to great swings of mood, one minute feeling happy and lighthearted, the next feeling downcast and dispirited? Do you sometimes start two jobs at a time because they are both equally important to you? Do you often change your mind if a new point of view suddenly appears? Perhaps this makes people think you are unreliable and volatile.

Scleranthus

If all this sounds familiar to you, then you are probably one of those people who easily lose their inner balance. Rather like rushes in the wind, you react to every argument, first leaning in one direction and then in another. Every new aspect of a situation, every new thought sets you doubting again. Thus, every decision becomes torture, above all when you seek to find the optimal solution for yourself. However, contrary to the Cerato type who also suffers from indecision, you do not seek advice.

You feel inwardly torn between two things

■ How your life can change for the better
Dr Bach's Scleranthus flower remedy can help stabilize your inner balance. It will make you less prone to mood swings and more sure of yourself when making decisions. Even though you will continue to see all the facets of a matter, you will be better able to make the decision that is right for you without long hesitation.

Star of Bethlehem

*Lift up your eyes and you will
see the stars.*
Philippine proverb

In cases of shock and its conse-quences Severe physical or emotional trauma – for example accident, injury or bad news – can trigger in us a state of shock. Physical and emotional blocks can be the consequences; in the short-term these manifest themselves in such symptoms as shaky knees, trembling, palpitations, outbreaks of perspiration, and even loss of consciousness.

Star of Bethlehem (or the Rescue Remedy, which contains Star of Bethlehem as well as other flower essences – see page 98) can be a real help in overcoming such shock situations. Taking this flower remedy will make it easier for you to deal with shock both physically and emotionally.

Some shock situations can lie far back in our past, sometimes up to decades ago, and have never really been properly "digested". Thus, the blocks caused at the time the shock happened are still disrupting the flow of energy and information in us without our being aware of this. The result can be that we suffer from such things as sleeplessness, heart and stomach troubles and back pain for which no cause can be found and which are frequently dismissed as disorders of the autonomic nervous system.

Star of Bethlehem

■ **How your life can change for the better**
In all these cases it would be worthwhile to try the Star of Bethlehem remedy. Dr Bach said of it, that it eases pain and sorrow, even if the cause lies a long time ago.

Star of Bethlehem makes it possible to "dissolve" the inner blockages so that our vital energy can once more flow through our bodies unhindered. The associated physical symptoms will then vanish all by themselves.

Sweet Chestnut

God does not send us despair to
kill us; he sends it to awaken
new life in us.
Hermann Hesse

Have you ever despaired in your life? Then you will know the
state of absolute hopelessness. With a feeling of helpless weakness,
you stand as if before a brick wall knowing that you can no longer
bear the burden you carry. You feel cut off from the world with all
its light and warmth. You have no strength left to do anything
more yourself.

Your situation appears hopeless to you

You should really be screaming your pain out loud, but that is
not generally possible. Instead, you barely voice a complaint about
the extreme situation you are in; you just try to be brave. In any
case, you are convinced that no-one can help you. Yet it is exactly
at this point that a chance exists to find a way out of your
desperate state.

This requires a willingness to talk to other people about
your feeling of helplessness. Through dialogue not only can
we find comfort, we can also gain new insights which might
point the way out of our despair. Sometimes situations like
this prove to be a turning point that forces us to adopt
a different attitude. For example, the partner of a drug
addict might recognize that separation is, for both
of them, the only possible way that also offers
the other a chance of returning to health.

■ **How your life can change for the better**
Whatever has triggered your desperation – whether
it was serious illness, the loss of a loved one, or the
long martyrdom of an unhappy relationship – the
Sweet Chestnut remedy can help you to find
renewed strength and hope, and to find a way
leading out of your darkness and despair to a
brighter, friendlier life.

Sweet
Chestnut

Complementary flowers (see page 22): Gentian, Willow, White Chestnut, Gorse, Pine

Vervain

You can lead someone on to the right path, but you cannot force him to stay on it.
Confucius

Do you tend to get very enthusiastic about a person or a task and to commit yourself even when it is almost beyond your strength? Is it important for you to convince others of things that you yourself find good? Are you often full of initiative and energy, overtaxing yourself physically in the process? Do you often feel tense and overstressed?

You are probably one of those energetic people who easily become enthusiastic about something and then work at it until they drop. It is not your way to change an opinion once you have formed it. You carry on with a task or a project right through to the end, displaying great perseverance and consistency. In doing so, you are not exactly gentle with yourself; permanent tension with few periods of rest is the rule. No wonder the day eventually comes when you feel the consequences of your strength-sapping behaviour – often in the form of cramped muscles and nervous exhaustion.

In your desire to carry others along with you, in your sheer enthusiasm, you often exaggerate and are prone to preach. In other words, you try to force your own opinion on others, saying: "This is the way you must do it".

Vervain

■ How your life can change for the better

Dr Bach's Vervain flower remedy can help you to treat yourself more gently. It can help you learn to recognize when you are putting other people under pressure with your enthusiasm, and how you overtax yourself and others. This flower remedy can support you while you try out new ways of behaving which will allow you the rest and relaxation that you need. Leave the work undone for once, or cancel an appointment, when you find you are tired and exhausted.

Complementary flowers (page 22): Impatiens, Beech, Rock Water

Vine

Woe to the power that buries its incumbent.
The Talmud

Are you able to see the overall picture, even in emergencies, taking command if necessary? Do you usually feel you are right in arguments? Are you good at giving orders? Do you make an assured and determined impression? Are you strong-willed and persevering?

Vine

Whether you think it or not, you are probably leader material. Equipped with a feeling for power and authority, you quickly take the lead in any group, deciding how things should be done. Perhaps you are active in a position of leadership already. In any case, you can generally get your own way, but you may give others the impression that you are rather unbending and strict.

Your relations with others only become difficult if you exaggerate and turn from being a capable, differentiating leader into a tyrant who issues orders, expecting them to be obeyed **You always** without argument. Then your feeling for what is the right course **want to be** of action could easily turn into insistence that you are right, and it **right** becomes no longer be a question of the matter in hand but of your own power and persona. In such a situation you can become dictatorial and overbearing, using your energy and abilities to make decisions that you insist others stick by.

Even if the tendency to pursue power is not very marked in you, or even if you are unaware of it, you would be well advised to take the Vine flower remedy at the smallest sign of despotic behaviour or a desire for power – above all, if you suffer greatly from tense muscles and stiff joints. According to Dr Bach, a wish to dominate manifests itself physically in these areas.

■ **How your life can change for the better**

Learn to accept others as partners
The Vine flower essence can help you to handle your innate leadership qualities so as to avoid using them to repress and dominate others. When delivering orders to others you always should bear in mind that you are dealing with human beings who also have souls and egos and are entitled to their own dignity. Your desire to dominate will perhaps be diminished and you will find you are better able to motivate and guide others without exerting undue pressure.

Complementary flowers (page 22): Impatiens, Beech, Rock Water

Walnut

Walnut

There is no point in arguing with those who follow a different path.
Confucius

Are you facing a far-reaching change in your life, such as a change of job or profession, separation from a partner, or departure from the parental home? Are you feeling untypically uncertain as to whether your decision is the right one to make?

You don't usually worry about other people's opinions but you are suddenly noticing that you can be influenced by the remarks of others, such as "Do you really want to leave this marvellous job?" Or, "You can't do this to your parents and go off and live in another town." You may become so unsure of yourself that you actually abandon your plans, despite feeling deep down that this is the right thing for you to do now. Perhaps as a result of your uncertainty you go on living at your parents' home, or you decide not to leave your partner. You know that you should be taking this step for your own good and to advance your personal development, but something holds you back.

You feel momentarily unsure of yourself

Emotions play an important role in decisions of this kind, since they usually entail giving up habits or links to which we are attached. This is not easy, so we swing back and forth in our attempt to reach a decision. At times like these we are particularly sensitive to outside influences, and these can make us even more uncertain of ourselves.

■ How your life can change for the better

In this kind of situation, Dr Bach's Walnut remedy can strengthen your powers of self-assertion. It helps you regain inner confidence and gives you the courage to take the step you have planned, irrespective of what others say.

Dr Bach described Walnut as the "link-breaker". The flower remedy can support you in letting go of emotional ties and give you the necessary defence against the disturbing influence of others. It increases your strength to follow your own way, independent of the opinion and the insistence of other people. With the help of Walnut, the difficulties that you face in the transition from one phase in your life to another can be minimized, no matter what stage of life you have reached. It can make teething easier for a baby, ease the confusion of puberty, alleviate the tensions and imbalances of the menopause, and help to approach retirement with pleasure and optimism.

Complementary flowers (page 22): Centaury, Wild Oat

Water Violet

*You may have all the advantages –
but if you lack humility, you will be
incomplete.*
Jewish saying

Water Violet

Do you sometimes feel lonely even in a crowd at a friend's
party? Do you find it difficult to get to know other people
quickly because you are reserved and distant? Do you prefer
to solve your own problems alone without making too much
fuss? Do you refuse to get involved in the affairs of others?
Then you are one of those people who often stand like a rock
amidst the waves, calm, in command and inwardly untouched
by the human – often far too human – confusion around you.

You prefer to keep your distance from others

No-one would think that you, too, might have problems
and worries because you never give any sign of them. Other
people consider you to be strong, if sometimes a little cool
and unapproachable. In fact, your reserve masks secret
feelings of pride and superiority which perhaps developed
because of exceptional ability and achievement, or perhaps
as a result of coming from a rich or aristocratic family.

The problem for many Water Violet types arises when a feeling
of justifiable pride turns into arrogance and superiority. Some of
them are apt to forget that the pre-conditions for their
achievements lie in inherited talents and opportunities. These
were a gift, and although what you have built on this foundation
should by all means be a source of pleasure and pride, it is not a
reason for treating others who are less fortunate in an arrogant or
superior manner.

■ **How your life can change for the better**

Dr Bach's Water Violet flower remedy can help you to reduce your
pride to an acceptable level. It can help you learn to moderate any
secret feelings of superiority. Water Violet will also help you to let
go of your inner reserve. You will then be better able to relate to
others and will feel less isolated.

Complementary flowers (page 22): Vervain, Vine, Beech, Impatiens

White Chestnut

Where clarity reigns there will be rest – or it will emerge gradually all by itself.
Wilhelm von Humboldt

Do you know how it feels for your thoughts to keep revolving round and round a particular subject, like a cracked record? Do you toss and turn at night, unable to "switch off"? Do you often not hear when spoken to because your thoughts are too busy with something else?

This "thought roundabout" is usually set going by events which arouse fear, worry or exasperation. For example, after an argument – or perhaps after an interview – thoughts of what we really wanted to say keep going through our minds; or before an examination we may take our anxieties onto the "thought roundabout".

Positive events as well as negative ones can set this unstoppable thought process in motion – planning a birthday party, for instance, or a forthcoming journey.

White Chestnut

A thought holds you fast

So long as the roundabout keeps turning we are incapable of thinking about anything else: we cannot concentrate, we become inattentive, and peace of mind and clarity of thought completely elude us. This results in us shutting off outside impulses: we are simply unable to register them. If this condition lasts for long, our general health can suffer. We lose sleep, and if negative thoughts get hold of us they can make us feel sad or even depressed.

■ **How your life can change for the better**
With the help of Dr Bach's White Chestnut remedy you can stop this thought roundabout. You will find with relief that peace and clarity of mind slowly return. You will regain your ability to absorb

Your "thought roundabout" comes to a halt outside information, you will once again be able to concentrate on what is happening in the present, and you will find you can sleep better at night.

It is generally useful to take White Chestnut in combination with flower remedies which will ease the feelings that triggered the churning thoughts in the first place – feelings of guilt, fear or jealousy, for example.

Complementary flowers (page 22): Pine, Holly, Mimulus, Sweet Chestnut, Rock Rose, Vervain, Honeysuckle, Clematis, Willow

Wild Oat

We demand that life have meaning;
but it will have just as much
meaning as we are able to give it.
Hermann Hesse

Wild Oat

Do people, situations or tasks soon bore you, even though at first you were full of enthusiasm for them? Do you often start something – whether at work, in your leisure, or in a relationship – but fail to see it through because you suddenly become unsure of whether it is right for you? Do you sometimes feel aimless, or that you don't know what you should be doing with your life? Is it difficult for you to decide on a career path because you fulfil the conditions for several professions?

Then you are probably one of those people who do not really know where they are going in life. In some ways you are constantly searching for something that will fulfil you and give you pleasure. You have tried all sorts of things but in the end you are always uncertain of whether it really is the right thing. Contrary to Scleranthus types, who find it hard to decide between two things, your difficulty lies in choosing what is right or important for you from a number of possibilities. This leads to feelings

You are often dissatisfied with your life

of dissatisfaction, in particular that somehow your life is slipping through your fingers.

■ **How your life can change for the better**

The Wild Oat flower remedy can help give direction to your life. To find your direction you must listen carefully to your "inner voice". Every person carries within them a source of information which knows exactly what is right and meaningful for their own personal development. The Wild Oat remedy will help you to get in touch with your own source, your inner voice, and this will make it easier for you to choose between the opportunities that lie before you. When you have succeeded in doing this, you will feel more confident in yourself and satisfied with life.

Wild Rose

When I bear a green twig in my heart, a song bird will come and perch on it.
Chinese proverb

Do you tend towards the opinion that a person cannot change anything in their life, that their character and fate are fixed, and therefore there is no point in trying to make things better? Do you sometimes feel a deep tiredness and lack of drive, and think "It's no good anyway"? Do you often feel sad at heart even though you have plenty to be happy about, for example when all is going well with you and your family, or when you have just seen or experienced something pleasant? This lack of joy is not really connected with actual sadness or depression; what you feel deep down inside is that somehow you are not properly sharing in the good things of life and are missing out.

    If these descriptions feel familiar to you, then it is likely that you are one of those people who do

Wild Rose

not stand up for themselves very decisively against life's difficulties, instead you just accept them with resignation. This kind of bending to Fate is sometimes confused with the feeling of being "above it all". But here inner joy and the feeling of being truly happy and content are missing.

Some people are barely conscious of this deep resignation in their lives. They might feel only an emptiness, a lack of joy which runs through their lives like a red thread. Or they might notice a feeling of apathy, that they lack interest in what is going on around them. They could be described as having "closed the shutters" against the outside world, and this attitude can often be traced back to early childhood experiences or a long illness.

You lack a little joy in living

■ How your life can change for the better

The Wild Rose flower remedy cannot change this sort of attitude from one day to the next. In some cases psychiatric therapy may be necessary. However, Wild Rose can give a person support while the "shutters" are carefully opened again. It is important that you become aware of your condition and learn to recognize that the state of crisis which initially led you to batten down the hatches probably no longer exists.

Where feelings of resignation have arisen through illness or other strokes of fate, Wild Rose remedy will help to make you "mobile" once more. It will also help you to realize that you can improve your situation by your actions, and do not have to just sit down and accept it.

Complementary flowers (page 22): Star of Bethlehem, Mustard, Gentian, Honeysuckle

Willow

*It is not what we experience but
what we feel about our experience
that decides our destiny.*
Marie von Ebner-Eschenbach

Do you often feel that you attract everything that is negative in
life? Do you sometimes ask yourself what you have done to
deserve all your problems? Are you one of those people for
whom everything goes wrong? Your car probably spends more
time at the garage than other people's seem to, and on holiday
you probably have to move at least once before you find an
You feel acceptable hotel. The list of unfortunate incidents in your life
Fate is seems endless, apparently proving repeatedly that you are one
unkind to of the people for whom things always go wrong, that Fate is not
you very kind to you.

Naturally, over time it is possible to become bitter about all this
bad luck and start to resent other people who seem to get on so
much easier in life. You might even stop expecting anything
positive to happen and count only on the negative.

What we now have here is a vicious circle – so long as we look at
the world negatively and view it with bitterness we shall go on
having negative experiences. This is because the negative attitude
and expectations inside us have a direct and an indirect effect on
other people's behaviour towards us. In the words of a German
proverb: "As the call rings out to the forest, so it echoes back."
If we approach people negatively or distrustfully, they can feel it
and this makes it difficult for them to react to us in a relaxed and
natural way, and this becomes our next negative experience.

During a long and serious illness it is particularly hard to avoid
becoming bitter and resentful, especially if we regard the illness as
yet another a stroke of Fate rather than a challenge leading to
change in our lives.

It will probably be hard for you to accept all this: you have
enough examples to prove you are an unusually frequent victim of
adverse circumstances. However, we all experience everyday
things that go wrong. The important thing is how we react to

them – whether we try to see the positive aspect of the situation. If, for example, an event I have been looking forward to for a long time – say a trip to the theatre or a concert – is cancelled at the last minute, I can react in one of two ways:

"Typical! Whenever I want to do something, it goes wrong!" OR

"What a pity! Still, I'll get a chance to listen to my new CD this evening."

■ **How your life can change for the better**
Willow flower remedy can help you learn to overcome your bitterness. When you succced in doing so you will see that you are co-responsible for your situation and are not just a victim of some "dark power". From this insight the possibility of changing things becomes real and you will find the strength to make the changes you want.

Complementary flowers (page 22): Gentian, Heather, Holly, Honeysuckle, Star of Bethlehem, Gorse

Willow

Self-treatment with Bach flowers

So far, this book has concentrated on explaining how to identify and select flower essences suitable for your own personal remedy mixture. This chapter answers questions about buying, using and storing flower remedies. Finally, it discusses the rescue remedy and its many uses.

How to use Bach flower remedies

This chapter includes all the information you need to treat yourself with Dr Bach's flower remedies. It has been carefully sub-divided to help you find important information, such as dosage instructions, quickly and easily.

When is treatment useful?

Dr Bach's remedies can be applied in many everyday situations to treat yourself, your children, and even your pets and plants:

■ In emergencies and cases of acute emotional stress

In acute cases By virtue of their simplicity and harmlessness, Bach flower remedies are particularly suitable for self-treatment in emergencies or cases of acute emotional stress in everyday life, such as examination nerves, the effects of emotional shock such as experienced in separation from or the loss of a loved one, a fear of flying or the aftermath of an accident. (See also the rescue remedy on page 98.)

■ In cases of longstanding emotional and physical disturbance
Here, too, self-treatment is in principle possible, although if there are physical symptoms you must discuss this with the doctor treating the case before embarking on any supporting therapy.

Support in cases of illness

Bach remedies can help to overcome the negative emotional symptoms connected with a chronic condition – such as lack of courage, despair and resentment – while also strengthening a person's optimism and courage to face life. Treatment requires some experience in the use of the remedies, as well as sensitivity and good powers of observation. It is always a good idea at the beginning of self-treatment to discuss matters with an experienced Bach flower practitioner.

■ **For ongoing personal development**

Working towards changing one's behaviour If we wish to rid ourselves of disruptive mannerisms and character weaknesses – such as intolerance, pride, envy, aggressiveness or feelings of inferiority – and find our way to inner calm and contentment, Bach flower remedies can be a significant help to us. A pre-condition to effective treatment, however, is honest self-analysis, a good amount of self-knowledge, and the ability to admit to one's own weaknesses.

■ **For children and infants**

Children react well and quickly Children react well and quickly to treatment with Bach flowers. The remedies can be helpful, for example, in cases of schooling difficulties, jealousy between siblings, homesickness and fears in general. In all these situations you can also use the rescue remedy (see page 98) as a first-aid measure. For further treatment, it is a good idea to consult a practitioner.

■ **Animals and plants**

Bach remedies have just as effective a healing, strengthening and calming effect as other plant remedies on sick and exhausted animals and plants.

Limits to self-treatment

Serious emotional problems are not appropriate for self-treatment. In cases of neuroses, psychoses, endogenous depression or deep-seated emotional problems and conflicts, you are best advised to consult an experienced therapist. This also applies in cases of severe physical illness where, after discussion with the doctor treating the illness, Bach remedies can be administered as a method of support.

A common but very different limit to self-treatment lies in the difficulty we all have in recognizing and accepting our own faults and personal weaknesses. For example, we might be unhappy because we feel misunderstood, but be quite unable to see that we perpetuate our state of mind through our own behaviour.

Admitting one's own weaknesses

Reactions to Bach flowers

Reactions when first taking Bach remedies vary from individual to individual:

● Some might experience an increased need for rest and sleep, perhaps accompanied with vivid dreams – a sign that things are moving on an emotional level. Others might feel more positive, more energetic, more stable emotionally, in fact more content right from the start of the treatment or in the course of just a few weeks.

Rapid improvement is often seen

● In rare cases there can initially be a worsening of the emotional or physical symptoms. If this happens, stop taking the remedy until this "healing" reaction has disappeared. Experience has shown that this will take a few hours, or at most a day or two. Subsequently, start taking the drops again, reducing the dosage slightly at first.

How long should a treatment last?

In acute situations

In serious acute conditions you will feel better relatively quickly, after perhaps a few hours or one or two days. You can stop taking the drops when you feel emotionally more settled or that you no longer need them.

● You should take your mixture for three or four weeks: this represents approximately the contents of a 30 ml treatment bottle. After this time, if you feel that the drops have done you good but that you still need them, you can repeat the mixture. Or you can compose a different mixture appropriate to your present condition. It can sometimes take a few months before you regain your old equilibrium.

● If you are using the flower remedies for ongoing personal development, or in the case of a longstanding condition, you will need to exercise more patience and encourage an inner willingness to cooperate actively in the healing process. According to the gravity of your condition, your age and the nature of your personality you might have to wait a year or more before a positive change stabilizes. This does not mean that you must wait so long for improvement. You should already begin to feel better within the first three or four weeks from commencing the treatment.

For ongoing personal development

Are there any side effects?

No physical or emotional secondary effects have thus far been observed in the use of Bach flower remedies.

Interaction with other medications

No interaction occurs with plant-based, homeopathic or chemical medicaments. An exception, however, are high-potency homeopathic preparations: generally, these are not taken at the same time as Bach flower remedies. If in any doubt, ask the person treating you for advice.

For patients taking psychopharmacological drugs

Patients supplementing psychopharmacological drugs with Bach remedies can sometimes decrease the drug dosage, carefully and gradually, in consultation with their doctor. After prolonged use of psychopharmacological drugs, Bach flower remedies usually have no effect.

Where to buy Bach flower remedies

Bach flower remedies are available in stock bottles from most health food shops and good chemists. If you have trouble finding them in your area, however, they can be obtained from the Edward Bach Centre at Wallingford in Oxfordshire, or from Nelson's or Ainsworth's homeopathic pharmacies in London, both of whom provide a mail order service (for addresses, see page 100). They can supply stock bottles, or make up a treatment to your own specification.

Available from health food shops and most chemists'

Preparing a treatment mixture

To prepare a treatment mixture yourself, you will need:

● A stock bottle of each of your chosen remedies;

● A 20 or 30 ml bottle with a dropper as your treatment bottle;

● Still, fresh or spring water (distilled or demineralized water is not suitable);

Alcohol or vinegar is used to conserve the mixture

● Either 45% vol. alcohol or a high-alcohol spirit such as cognac, brandy etc. Liquers are not suitable. Fruit vinegar can be used in remedies for children and all those who cannot tolerate alcohol.

Diluting and conserving your treatment mixture

For regular use the concentrated essence in the stock bottles is diluted in the treatment bottle in the following proportion:

● 1 drop of concentrate of each flower remedy to 10 ml of solution. That is to say, if you are preparing a 20 ml treatment bottle mixture, put 2 drops from each stock bottle into the treatment bottle; for a 30 ml bottle, put in 3 drops from each stock bottle.

Fill the treatment bottle three-quarters full with water, then top up the other quarter with alcohol or vinegar.

Mixing flower essences

You can mix the flower remedies as you wish. If, for example, you have chosen five flower remedies and wish to prepare your mixture in a 30 ml bottle, put 3 drops of each remedy into the treatment bottle; that would be 5 x 3 drops = 15 drops in total. Fill the bottle three-quarters full with water, then fill up the remaining quarter with your chosen conserving agent.

Storing and keeping properties

The stock bottles containing the concentrates can be kept for a virtually unlimited period of time. They should be stored at room temperature and protected against light.

The treatment bottle containing your personal remedy mixture should not be kept longer than three to four weeks. As soon as the appearance or taste of the contents changes you should dispose of them.

How to take the remedies

Standard dosage

● The standard dose from your treatment bottle is 4 drops taken 4 times daily, either directly on the tongue or from a plastic spoon. In acute cases, 4 drops may be taken hourly until you feel better, if necessary for two or three days.

You should consider these dosage instructions as guidelines only. In self-treatment, you should allow your own feelings to decide how many drops to take and how often. Because of the nature of the flower remedies there is no possibility of an "overdose".

● The drops are best taken on waking, at noon, in the afternoon, and on retiring. The remedies work best if held for a moment in the mouth before swallowing. The drops should be taken away from food and drink.

What if there is no effect?

If you have been taking your mixture for four to six weeks and feel no effect, this may be due to one or more of the following reasons:

Assessing the situation

● The mixture is unsuitable. Reconsider your symptoms list (see pages 17 to 21) and compare it again with the repertory and the flower descriptions to find the flower essences that suit you.

● You are expecting too much and have therefore failed to notice subtle changes.

● The willingness to change your emotional symptoms is lacking at a subconscious level.

● Your ability to react is blocked by psycho-pharmacological drugs. In this case you should talk to an experienced practitioner about how to proceed: do not just dismiss the Bach remedies as generally ineffective.

Ask a specialist

The rescue remedy

The rescue remedy is a combination of five flower essences that Dr Bach discovered and composed himself. The mixture contains the following flowers:

- Star of Bethlehem, Rock Rose, Impatiens, Cherry Plum and Clematis.

Rescue remedy can be obtained wherever Bach flower remedies are sold.

When to use the rescue remedy

The rescue remedy is used as a form of "first aid" in situations which cause great stress. For example, before a visit to the dentist, before an examination, in cases of stage fright and fear of flying, after receiving bad news, on the loss of a loved one or in cases of separation.

■ The rescue remedy is meant for acute situations and should not be taken for longer than two or three days. If a stressful situation lasts longer than this, it is more beneficial to prepare a "personal" emergency mixture suited to the prevailing emotional symptoms. In principle, however, you can take the rescue remedy as often as needed because, like all Bach flower remedies, it is completely harmless.

■ The rescue remedy is a reliable form of "first aid" in cases of injury, for example minor cuts and burns, operations, the physical consequences of accidents such as sprains and bruises. It stabilizes the emotional balance, often taking effect after just a few minutes.

■ The rescue remedy can be used for adults, children and babies.

Please note

The rescue remedy cannot replace any necessary medical attention.

How to use the rescue remedy

The rescue remedy can be used both internally and externally.

Internal Use

The water glass method

● In acute cases put 4 drops of the essence from a stock bottle into a small glass (20 ml) and fill it up with still water, juice or tea. Drink this solution in sips over a period of 15 minutes. If you feel no effect from the first glass, you may take a second and even a third.

● Many people take the rescue remedy undiluted when needed, either by dropping it directly onto the tongue or by licking it from the back of the hand. Two drops are sufficient in this case.

Can be taken undiluted

● If a person is unconscious it is best to give the drops in undiluted form: 2 to 3 drops are dripped onto the lips or gums.

● For children and small babies, put 4 drops of the concentrate in a 20 ml bottle with a dropper and fill it with still water. Dribble 4 drops of this solution at short intervals onto the lips or tongue.

External Use

For cases of tension, minor burns and injuries, and for skin problems.

● Put 6 drops from the stock bottle in half a litre of water and use this to make compresses.

Bach rescue cream

The Edward Bach Centre in Wallingford makes a cream based on the rescue remedy, with the extra addition of Crab Apple flower essence. Rescue cream is available wherever Bach flower remedies are on sale.

For all small injuries

Particularly suitable for treating small injuries, the cream quickly sets off a healing process in the case of, for example, small cuts, minor burns, sunburn, sprains and bruises.

Further reading

Bach, Dr Edward: *The Collected Writing of Edward Bach*, Bach Educational Programmes

Bach, Dr Edward: *The Twelve Healers and Other Remedies*, The C W Daniel Company Ltd, Saffron Waldon

Bach, Dr Edward: *Heal Thyself*, The C W Daniel Company Ltd

Barnard, Julian: *A Guide to the Bach Flower Remedies*, The C W Daniel Company Ltd

Chancellor, Philip M: *Handbook of the Bach Flower Remedies*, The C W Daniel Company Ltd

Evans, Jane: *Introduction to the Benefits of the Bach Flower Remedies*, The C W Daniel Company Ltd

Hyne Jones, T W: *Dictionary of the Bach Flower Remedies*, The C W Daniel Company Ltd

Vlamis, Gregory: *Flowers to the Rescue*, Thorsons Publishing Group, Wellingborough

Wheeler, F J: *The Bach Remedies Repertory*, The C W Daniel Company Ltd

Weeks, Nora: *The Medical Discoveries of Edward Bach, Physician*, The C W Daniel Company Ltd

Weeks, Nora/Bullen, Victor: *The Bach Flower Remedies, Illustration and Preparation*, The C W Daniel Company Ltd

Useful addresses

The Dr Edward Bach Centre
Mount Vernon
Sotwell
Wallingford
Oxfordshire OX10 0P2
Tel: 01491 833712

Mail order services:

Nelson Homeopathic Pharmacy
73 Duke Street
London W1M 6BY
Tel: 0171 495 2404

Ainsworths Pharmacy
36 New Cavendish Street
London W1M 7LH

Healing Herbs Ltd
P.O. Box 65
Hereford HR2 0DW

Index

First published under the title "Innere Harmonie durch Bach Blüten" by Gräfe und Unzer Verlag GmbH, Munich
© 1994 Gräfe und Unzer

Authorized English language edition published by Time-Life Books BV, 1066 AZ Amsterdam
© 1997 Time-Life Books BV
First English language printing 1997

English translation by Kay Gillioz MIL MTA
Editor: Christine Noble
Layout and DTP: Dawn McGinn

PHOTOS
Front cover: Michael Nischke
Back cover: Hans Reinhard
6-7 and 38-39: Hermann Eisenbeiss
90-91: Reiner Schmitz

ISBN 0 7054 3501 6

20 19 18 17 16 15 14 13 12 11 10 9 8 7 6 5 4 3 2 1